W9-CFL-434

Commercial
Oral Exam Guide

by Michael D. Hayes

Seventh Edition

The comprehensive
guide to prepare you
for the FAA checkride

Aviation Supplies & Academics, Inc.
Newcastle, Washington

Commercial Oral Exam Guide
Seventh Edition
by Michael D. Hayes

Aviation Supplies & Academics, Inc.
7005 132nd Place SE
Newcastle, Washington 98059-3153

Go to **www.asa2fly.com/reader/oegc** for further resources associated with this book. Also, visit the ASA website often (**www.asa2fly.com**, Product Updates link or search "OEG-C") to find updates posted there due to FAA regulation revisions that may affect this book.

© 1992–2010 Aviation Supplies & Academics, Inc.
All rights reserved. Seventh Edition published 2010.

No part of this book shall be reproduced, stored in any retrieval system, or transmitted by any means, electronic, mechanical, xerographic, audio/visual record, or otherwise, without the written permission from the publisher. While every precaution has been taken in the preparation of this book, the publisher and Michael D. Hayes assume no responsibility for errors or omissions. Neither is any liability assumed for damages resulting from the use of the information contained herein. None of the material in this guide supersedes any documents, procedures, or regulations issued by the Federal Aviation Administration.

ASA-OEG-C7
ISBN 1-56027-796-3
       978-1-56027-796-5

Printed in the United States of America
2013   2012   9   8   7   6   5   4   3

Library of Congress Cataloging-in-Publication Data
Hayes, Michael D.
      Commercial oral exam guide / by Michael D. Hayes.
            p.   cm.
      "ASA-OEG-C"—T.p. verso.
      1. Aeronautics—Examinations, questions, etc. 2. Aeronautics,
      Commercial—Examinations, questions, etc. 3. United States.
      Federal Aviation Administration—Examinations—Study guides.
      4. Oral examinations. I. Title.
      TL546.5.H35   1992
      629.132'5217'076—dc20   92-36217
                                                CIP

This guide is dedicated to the many talented students, pilots, and flight instructors I have had the opportunity to work with over the years. Also, special thanks to Mark Hayes and many others who supplied the patience, encouragement, and understanding necessary to complete the project.

— M.D.H.

Contents

Introduction

The *Commercial Oral Exam Guide* is a comprehensive guide designed for pilots who are involved in training for the Commercial Pilot Certificate. It was originally designed for use in a Part 141 flight school but quickly became popular with those training under 14 CFR Part 61 who are not affiliated with an approved school. The guide will also prove beneficial to pilots who wish to refresh their knowledge or who are preparing for a flight review.

The Commercial Pilot Practical Test Standards book (FAA-S-8081-12B) specifies the areas in which knowledge must be demonstrated by the applicant before issuance of a pilot certificate or rating. The *Commercial Oral Exam Guide* is designed to evaluate a pilot's knowledge of those areas.

Commercial pilots are professionals engaged in various flight activities for compensation or hire. Because of their professional status, they should exhibit a significantly higher level of knowledge than a private pilot. This guide assumes that the pilot has the prerequisite knowledge necessary for Private Pilot Certification and attempts to cover only those advanced areas of knowledge necessary for Commercial Pilot Certification.

In this guide, questions and answers are organized into nine chapters which represent those areas of knowledge required for the practical test. At any time during the practical test, an examiner may ask questions pertaining to any of the subject areas within these divisions. Through intensive post-commercial-checkride debriefings, we have provided you with the most consistent questions asked, along with the information necessary for a knowledgeable response.

The guide may be supplemented with other comprehensive study materials as noted in parentheses after each question. For example: (FAA-H-8083-25). The abbreviations for these materials and their titles are listed on the next page. Be sure that you use the latest revision of these references when reviewing for the test. Also, check the ASA website at **www.asa2fly.com** to see if any updates are posted within our Product Support pages; all the latest changes in FAA procedures and regulations that affect these questions will be listed there. In addition to the regular question-and-answer sessions in each chapter, questions for further review have been included at the end of sections. These additional questions are designed to be good study aids for the references below, upon which they are based.

14 CFR Part 23	*Airworthiness Standards: Normal, Utility, Acrobatic, and Commuter Category Airplanes*
14 CFR Part 43	*Maintenance, Preventive Maintenance, Rebuilding, and Alteration*
14 CFR Part 61	*Certification: Pilots, Flight Instructors, and Ground Instructors*
14 CFR Part 91	*General Operating and Flight Rules*
NTSB Part 830	*Notification and Reporting of Aircraft Accidents and Incidents*
FAA-H-8083-1	*Aircraft Weight and Balance Handbook*
FAA-H-8083-3	*Airplane Flying Handbook*
FAA-H-8083-9	*Aviation Instructor's Handbook*
FAA-H-8083-15	*Instrument Flying Handbook*
FAA-H-8083-25	*Pilot's Handbook of Aeronautical Knowledge*
FAA-P-8740-2	*Density Altitude*
FAA-P-8740-13	*Engine Operation for Pilots*
FAA-P-8740-41	*Medical Facts for Pilots*
FAA-S-8081-12	*Commercial Pilot Practical Test Standards for Airplane*
AC 00-6	*Aviation Weather*
AC 00-45	*Aviation Weather Services*
AC 00-54	*Pilot Windshear Guide*
AC 20-32	*Carbon Monoxide (CO) Contamination in Aircraft*
AC 25-14	*High Lift and Drag Devices*
AC 60-6B	*Airplane Flight Manuals (AFM), Approved Manual Materials, Markings, and Placards—Airplanes*
AC 61-65	*Certification: Pilots and Flight Instructors*
AC 61-67C	*Stall and Spin Awareness Training*

AC 65-12	*Airframe & Powerplant Mechanics: Powerplant Handbook*
AC 65-15	*Airframe & Powerplant Mechanics: Airframe Handbook*
AC 67-2	*Medical Handbook for Pilots*
AC 91-13	*Cold Weather Operation of Aircraft*
AC 91-33	*Use of Alternate Grades of Aviation Gasoline*
AC 91-67	*Minimum Equipment Requirements for General Aviation Operations under 14 CFR Part 91*
AC 120-12	*Private Carriage vs. Common Carriage of Persons or Property*
FSAT 00-09	*Increased Surveillance and Testing of Surface Movement Operations*
Order 7930.2	*Notices to Airmen Handbook*
Order 8900.1	*Flight Standards Information Management System*
AIM	*Aeronautical Information Manual*
A/FD	*Airport/Facility Directory*
NOTAMs	*Notices to Airmen*
P/CG	*Pilot/Controller Glossary* (from AIM)
POH	*Pertinent Pilot Operating Handbooks*
AFM	*Airplane Flight Manuals*

Note: Be sure that you use the latest revision of these references when reviewing for the checkride.

A review of the information presented within this guide along with a general review of the *Private Oral Exam Guide* (ASA-OEG-P) should provide the necessary preparation for the oral section of an FAA Commercial Pilot checkride or recertification check.

Certificates
and Documents

1

A. Privileges and Limitations

1. What privileges apply to a commercial pilot?
(14 CFR 61.133)

A person who holds a commercial pilot certificate may act as pilot-in-command of an aircraft:

a. Carrying persons or property for compensation or hire

b. For compensation or hire

Note: 14 CFR §61.133 also states that a commercial pilot must be qualified and comply with the applicable parts of the regulations that apply to the particular operation being conducted, for example Part 91 or 135.

2. Discuss commercial pilot operations.

A commercial pilot intending to conduct operations as a pilot-in-command of an aircraft carrying persons or property for compensation or hire should look cautiously at any proposal for revenue operating flights.

The following facts should be considered:

a. Part 61 states that you may be paid for acting as PIC of an aircraft engaged in carrying persons or property for compensation or hire. Part 61 does not mention, that if acting totally by yourself, you could be considered a commercial operator, and as such, be subject to an entirely different set of regulations.

b. A commercial pilot certificate by itself does not allow you to act as a commercial operator. It only allows you to work for a commercial operator and be paid for your service, with certain exceptions.

c. As a commercial pilot certain commercial operations are allowed without being in possession of an "Operating Certificate." Examples of such operations are: student instruction, certain nonstop sightseeing flights, ferry or training flights, aerial work operations including crop dusting, banner towing, aerial photography, powerline or pipeline patrol, etc. These operations are listed in 14 CFR §119.1.

3. What does the term "commercial operator" refer to? (14 CFR Part 1)

Commercial operator means a person who, for compensation or hire, engages in the carriage by aircraft in air commerce of persons or property, other than as an air carrier or foreign air carrier or under the authority of Part 375 of this title [Title 14]. Where it is doubtful that an operation is for "compensation or hire," the test applied is whether the carriage by air is merely incidental to the person's other business or is, in itself, a major enterprise for profit.

4. Define the term "common carriage." (AC 120-12A)

Common carriage refers to the carriage of passengers or cargo as a result of advertising the availability of the carriage to the public. A carrier becomes a common carrier when it "holds itself out" to the public, or a segment of the public, as willing to furnish transportation within the limits of its facilities to any person who wants it. There are four elements in defining a "common carrier":

a. A holding out or a willingness to

b. Transport persons or property

c. From place to place

d. For compensation.

5. Define "holding out." (AC 120-12A)

Holding out implies offering to the public the carriage of persons and property for hire either intrastate or interstate. This holding out which makes a person a common carrier can be done in many ways, and it does not matter how it is done.

a. Signs and advertising are the most direct means of holding out but are not the only ones.

b. A holding out may be accomplished through the actions of agents, agencies, or salesmen who may obtain passenger traffic from the general public and collect them into groups to be carried by the operator.

c. Physically holding out without advertising, yet gaining a reputation to "serve all," is sufficient to constitute an offer to carry all customers. For example, the expression of willingness to all customers with whom contact is made that the operator can and will perform the requested service is sufficient. It makes no difference if the holding out generates little success; the issue is the nature and character of the operation.

d. A carrier holding itself out as generally willing to carry only certain kinds of traffic is nevertheless a common carrier.

6. Define the term "private carriage." (AC 120-12A)

Carriage for hire that does not involve holding out is "private carriage." Private carriage for hire is carriage for one or several selected customers, generally on a long-term basis. The number of contracts must not be too great, otherwise it implies a willingness to make a contract with anybody. A carrier operating with 18 to 24 contracts has been labeled a common carrier because it has held itself out to serve the general public to the extent of its facilities. Private carriage has been found in cases where three contracts have been the sole basis of the operator's business. But the number of contracts is not the determining factor when assessing whether a particular operation is common carriage or private carriage; any proposal for revenue-generating flights that would most likely require certification as an air carrier should be examined closely if you intend to practice private carriage.

7. State some typical examples of private carriage operations. (Order 8900.1)

a. Carriage of the operator's own employees or property.

b. Carriage of participating members of a club.

c. Carriage of persons and property that is only incidental to the operator's primary business enterprise.

d. Carriage of persons or property for compensation or hire under a contractual business arrangement between the operator and another person or organization, which did not result from the operator's holding out or offering service. (In this situation the customer seeks an operator to perform the desired service and enters into an exclusive mutual agreement, as opposed to the operator seeking customers.)

8. **Determine if either of the following two scenarios are common carriage operations and, if so, why?**

   Scenario 1: I am a local businessman and require a package to be flown to a distant destination ASAP. I will pay you to fly my airplane to deliver this package.

   Scenario 2: I am a local businessman and require a package to be flown to a distant destination ASAP. You reply that you can do the job for a fee. You promptly line up a local rental aircraft you're checked out in and deliver the package.

   Scenario 2 would be considered a common carriage operation because you are holding out by indicating a general willingness to all customers with whom contact is made to transport persons or property from place to place for compensation.

9. **Briefly describe 14 CFR Parts 119, 121, 125, 135, and 137.**

   Part 119—Certification: Air Carriers and Commercial Operators

   Part 121—Operating Requirements: Domestic, Flag, and Supplemental Operations

   Part 125— Certification and Operations: Airplanes having a seating capacity of 20 or more passengers or a maximum payload capacity of 6,000 pounds or more

   Part 135— Operating Requirements: Commuter and On-Demand Operations

   Part 137—Agricultural Aircraft Operations

10. **What limitation is imposed on a newly certificated commercial airplane pilot if that person does not hold an instrument rating?** (14 CFR 61.133)

    The pilot must hold an instrument rating in the same category and class, or the Commercial Pilot Certificate that is issued is endorsed with a limitation prohibiting the following:

    a. The carriage of passengers for hire in airplanes on cross-country flights in excess of 50 nautical miles;

    b. The carriage of passengers for hire in airplanes at night.

11. **To act as pilot-in-command or in any other capacity as a required flight crewmember of a civil aircraft, what must a pilot have in his/her physical possession or readily accessible in the aircraft?** (14 CFR 61.3)

    a. A valid pilot certificate

    b. A photo identification

    c. A current and appropriate medical certificate

12. **If a certificated pilot changes his/her permanent mailing address and fails to notify the FAA Airman Certification branch of the new address, the pilot is entitled to exercise the privileges of the pilot certificate for what period of time?** (14 CFR 61.60)

    30 days after the date of the move.

13. **If a pilot certificate were accidentally lost or destroyed, a pilot could continue to exercise privileges of that certificate provided he/she follows what specific procedure?** (14 CFR 61.29)

    a. An application for the replacement of a lost or destroyed airman certificate issued under Part 61 is made by letter to the Department of Transportation, Federal Aviation Administration; and

    b. A person who has lost a certificate may obtain a facsimile from the FAA confirming that it was issued. The facsimile may be carried as a certificate for up to 60 days pending receipt of a duplicate certificate.

14. **To act as pilot-in-command of a high-performance aircraft, what flight experience requirements must be met?** (14 CFR 61.31)

    A high-performance airplane is an airplane with an engine of more than 200 horsepower. To act as pilot-in-command of a high-performance airplane a person must have:

    a. Received and logged ground and flight training from an authorized instructor in a high-performance airplane, or in a flight simulator or flight training device that is representative of a high-performance airplane; and

    Continued...

b. Been found proficient in the operation and systems of the airplane; and

c. Received a one-time endorsement in the pilot's logbook from an authorized instructor who certifies the person is proficient to operate a high-performance airplane.

15. To act as pilot-in-command of a pressurized aircraft, what flight experience requirements must be met? (14 CFR 61.31)

To act as pilot-in-command of a pressurized aircraft (an aircraft that has a service ceiling or maximum operating altitude, whichever is lower, above 25,000 feet MSL), a person must have received and logged ground and flight training from an authorized instructor and obtained an endorsement in the person's logbook or training record from an authorized instructor who certifies the person has:

a. satisfactorily accomplished the ground training which includes high-altitude aerodynamics, meteorology, respiration, hypoxia, etc.; and

b. received and logged training in a pressurized aircraft, or in a flight simulator or flight training device representative of a pressurized aircraft, and obtained an endorsement in the person's logbook or training record from an authorized instructor who found the person proficient in the operation of pressurized aircraft (must include normal cruise flight above 25,000 feet MSL, emergency procedures for rapid decompression, emergency descent procedures).

16. To act as pilot-in-command of a tailwheel airplane, what flight experience requirements must be met? (14 CFR 61.31)

No person may act as pilot-in-command of a tailwheel airplane unless that person has received and logged flight training from an authorized instructor in a tailwheel airplane and received an endorsement in the person's logbook from an authorized instructor who found the person proficient in the operation of a tailwheel airplane. The flight training must include at least the following maneuvers and procedures: normal and crosswind takeoffs and landings, wheel landings and go-around procedures.

17. When would a commercial pilot be required to hold a type rating? (14 CFR 61.31)

According to 14 CFR §61.31, a person who acts as a pilot-in-command of any of the following aircraft, must hold a type rating for that aircraft:

a. Large aircraft (gross weight over 12,500 pounds, except lighter-than-air)

b. Turbojet-powered airplanes

c. Other aircraft specified by the Administrator through aircraft type certificate procedures.

18. With respect to certification, privileges, and limitations of airmen, define the terms "Category," "Class" and "Type." (14 CFR Part 1)

Category—a broad classification of aircraft; i.e., airplane, rotor-craft, glider, etc.

Class—a classification of aircraft within a category having similar operating characteristics; i.e., single-engine land, multi-engine land, etc.

Type—a specific make and basic model of aircraft including modifications that do not change its handling or flight characteristics; i.e., DC-9, B-737, etc.

19. Can a pilot with a commercial certificate and multi-engine land rating carry passengers in a single-engine airplane? (14 CFR 61.31)

No. Unless the pilot holds a category, class and type rating (if a class and type rating is required) that applies to that aircraft, he or she may not act as pilot-in-command in this situation.

20. Can a commercial pilot carry a passenger in an aircraft operated in formation flight? (14 CFR 91.111)

No person may operate an aircraft, carrying passengers for hire, in formation flight.

21. Can a commercial pilot carry passengers in a restricted, limited or experimental category aircraft? (14 CFR 91.313, 91.315, 91.317, and 91.319)

No person may operate a restricted, limited, or experimental category aircraft carrying persons or property for hire.

22. When may a commercial pilot log flight time as second-in-command time? (14 CFR 61.51)

According to 14 CFR §61.51, a pilot may log second-in-command time only for that flight time during which that person:

a. Is qualified according to the second-in-command requirements of 14 CFR §61.55, and occupies a crewmember station in an aircraft that requires more than one pilot by the aircraft's type certificate; or

b. Holds the appropriate category, class, and instrument rating (if an instrument rating is required for the flight) for the aircraft being flown, and more than one pilot is required under the type certification of the aircraft or the regulations under which the flight is being conducted.

23. You are currently en route to your destination and the sun has set. When can you begin logging flight time as "night" flight time? (14 CFR Part 1)

"Night" is defined as the time between the end of evening civil twilight and the beginning of morning civil twilight, as published in the American Air Almanac and converted to local time. All flight time that occurs during this period of time is considered "night" flight time.

B. Currency Requirements

1. What are the requirements to remain current as a commercial pilot? (14 CFR 61.56 and 61.57)

a. To remain current a commercial pilot must have accomplished a flight review given in an aircraft for which that pilot is rated by an appropriately-rated instructor within the preceding 24 calendar months.

b. To carry passengers, a pilot must have made within the preceding 90 days:

- Three takeoffs and three landings as the sole manipulator of the flight controls of an aircraft of the same category and class and, if a type rating is required, of the same type.

- If the aircraft is a tailwheel airplane, the landings must have been made to a full stop.

- If operations are to be conducted during the period beginning 1 hour after sunset or 1 hour before sunrise, with passengers on board, the pilot-in-command must have made at least three takeoffs and three landings to a full stop during that period in an aircraft of the same category, class, and type (if a type rating is required).

Note: A person may act as pilot-in-command of a flight under day VFR or day IFR if no persons or property are carried if the flight review is current.

2. What class of medical certificate is required for commercial pilots? (14 CFR 61.23)

A second-class medical certificate is required in order to exercise commercial pilot privileges.

3. What is the duration of a second-class medical certificate for operations requiring a commercial pilot certificate? (14 CFR 61.23)

A second-class medical certificate expires at the end of the last day of the 12th month after the month of the date of the examination shown on the certificate for operations requiring a commercial certificate.

4. Is a commercial pilot required to log all flight time?
(14 CFR 61.51)

Each person must document and record, in a manner acceptable to
the Administrator, the training and aeronautical experience used to
meet the requirements for a certificate, rating or flight review of
this part. They must also document and record the aeronautical
experience required for meeting the recent flight experience
requirements of this part.

C. Aircraft Certificates and Documents

**1. What documents are required on board an aircraft prior
to flight?** (14 CFR 91.9 and 91.203)

A irworthiness Certificate

R egistration Certificate

O perating limitations — may take the form of an FAA-approved
AFM/POH, placards, instrument markings, or any combination
of the above.

W eight and balance data

**2. Which documents, required on board an aircraft, must
be displayed in such a way so as to be visible by both
passengers and crew?** (14 CFR 91.203)

No person may operate a civil aircraft unless the Airworthiness
Certificate required or a special flight authorization issued is displayed at the cabin entrance or cockpit entrance so that it is legible
to passengers and crew.

**3. Are the aircraft and engine logbooks required to be
carried on board an aircraft?**

No. Generally, it is more advisable to keep the logbooks in a safe,
secure place such as the office, home, etc. The regulations do not
specifically state where the logbooks are to be kept, but they do say
that they should be made available upon request.

4. How can a pilot determine if his/her aircraft is equipped with a Mode C altitude encoding transponder?

By referencing the current weight and balance equipment list for that aircraft, a pilot could positively determine if a Mode C transponder is installed.

5. If the Airworthiness Certificate of a particular aircraft indicated one of the following categories, what significance would this have? (14 CFR Part 23)

a. Normal Category

b. Utility Category

a. *Normal category*—Aircraft structure capable of withstanding a load factor of 3.8 Gs without structural failure. Applicable to aircraft intended for non-aerobatic operation.

b. *Utility category*—Aircraft structure must be capable of with-standing a load factor of 4.4 Gs. This would usually permit limited aerobatics, including spins (if approved for the aircraft).

6. Are airplane flight manuals (AFM) required to be on board all aircraft? (AC 60-6B)

14 CFR §91.9 requires that all U.S.-registered aircraft have available in the aircraft a current, approved AFM, or if applicable, any combination of approved manual materials, markings, and placards. Generally, all aircraft manufactured after March 1, 1979 must have an AFM. For airplanes type-certificated at gross weights of 6,000 pounds or under which were not required to have an AFM, the required information may be an AFM or any combination of approved manual material, markings, and placards. These materials must be current and available in the airplane during operation.

7. What are Special Flight Permits, and when are they necessary? (FAA-H-8083-25, 14 CFR 21.197)

It is an authorization that may be issued for an aircraft that may not currently meet applicable airworthiness requirements but is safe for a specific flight. These permits (possibly, following an inspection by an inspector) are typically issued for the following purposes:

a. Flying an aircraft to a base where repairs, alterations or maintenance are to be performed.

b. Delivering or exporting an aircraft.

c. Production flight testing new production aircraft.

d. Evacuating aircraft from areas of impending danger.

e. Conducting customer demonstration flights in new production aircraft that have satisfactorily completed production flight tests.

f. To allow the operation of an overweight aircraft for flight beyond its normal range over water or land areas where adequate landing facilities or fuel is not available.

8. What is the procedure for obtaining a special flight permit? (FAA-H-8083-25)

If a special flight permit is needed, assistance and the necessary forms may be obtained from the local FSDO or Designated Airworthiness Representative (DAR).

9. What instruments and equipment are required for VFR day flight? (14 CFR 91.205)

Required for VFR flight during the day:

a. Airspeed indicator

b. Altimeter

c. Magnetic direction indicator (compass)

d. Tachometer for each engine

e. Oil pressure gauge for each engine

f. Temperature gauge for each liquid-cooled engine

g. Oil temperature gauge for each air-cooled engine

h. Manifold pressure gauge for each altitude engine

i. Fuel gauge indicating the quantity in each tank

j. Landing gear position indicator

k. Flotation gear (if operated for hire over water beyond power-off gliding distance from shore)

l. Safety belts (approved metal-to-metal latching device for each occupant over 2 years old)

m. Shoulder harnesses (for each front seat if aircraft manufactured after 1978)

n. Emergency locator transmitter

10. What instruments and equipment are required for VFR night flight? (14 CFR 91.205)

Required for VFR flight at night:

a. Instruments and equipment required for VFR day flight.

b. Approved position lights (navigation lights).

c. An approved aviation red or aviation white anticollision light system.

d. If the aircraft is operated for hire, one electric landing light.

e. An adequate source of electrical energy for all installed electrical and radio equipment.

f. One spare set of fuses, or three spare fuses of each kind required that are accessible to the pilot in flight.

D. Aircraft Maintenance Requirements

1. Who is responsible for ensuring that an aircraft is maintained in an airworthy condition? (14 CFR 91.403)

The owner or operator of an aircraft is primarily responsible for maintaining an aircraft in an airworthy condition.

2. After aircraft inspections have been made and defects have been repaired, who is responsible for determining that the aircraft is in an airworthy condition? (14 CFR 91.7)

The pilot-in-command of a civil aircraft is responsible for determining whether that aircraft is in condition for safe flight. The pilot-in-command shall discontinue the flight when unairworthy mechanical, electrical, or structural conditions occur.

3. Can you legally fly an aircraft that has an inoperative flap position indicator?

Unless operations are conducted under 14 CFR §91.213, the regulations require that all equipment installed on an aircraft in compliance with either the Airworthiness Standards or the Operating Rules must be operative. If equipment originally installed in the aircraft is no longer operative, the Airworthiness Certificate is not valid until such equipment is either repaired or removed from that aircraft. However, the rules also permit the publication of a Minimum Equipment List (MEL) where compliance with these equipment requirements is not necessary in the interest of safety under all conditions.

4. Can an aircraft operator allow flight operations to be conducted in an aircraft with known inoperative equipment? (AC 91-67, 14 CFR 91.213)

Part 91 describes acceptable methods for the operation of an aircraft with certain inoperative instruments and equipment which are not essential for safe flight. These acceptable methods of operation are:

1. Operation of aircraft with a Minimum Equipment List (MEL), as authorized by 14 CFR §91.213(a).

2. Operation of aircraft without a MEL under 14 CFR §91.213(d).

5. What are Minimum Equipment Lists? (AC 91-67)

The Minimum Equipment List (MEL) is a precise listing of instruments, equipment, and procedures that allows an aircraft to be operated under specific conditions with inoperative equipment. The MEL is the specific inoperative equipment document for a particular make and model aircraft by serial and registration numbers; e.g., BE-200, N12345. The FAA-approved MEL includes only those items of equipment which the administrator finds may be inoperative and yet maintain an acceptable level of safety by appropriate conditions and limitations.

6. If an aircraft is not being operated under a MEL, how can you determine which instruments and equipment on board can be inoperative and the aircraft still be legal for flight? (14 CFR 91.213)

A person may takeoff an aircraft in operations conducted under Part 91 with inoperative instruments and equipment without an approved Minimum Equipment List provided the inoperative instruments and equipment are not—

a. Part of the VFR-day type certification instruments and equipment prescribed in the applicable airworthiness regulations under which the aircraft was type certificated;

b. Indicated as required on the aircraft's equipment list, or on the Kinds of Operations Equipment List, for the kind of flight operation being conducted;

c. Required by §91.205 or any other rule of this part for the specific kind of flight operation being conducted;

d. Required to be operational by an airworthiness directive.

7. What is an aircraft equipment list, and where is it found? (FAA-H-8083-1)

Furnished with the aircraft is an equipment list that specifies all the required equipment, and all equipment approved for installation in the aircraft. The weight and arm of each item is included on the list, and all equipment installed when the aircraft left the factory is checked. It is usually found with the weight and balance data.

8. What must happen if an AMT removes or installs a piece of equipment that is on the aircraft equipment list? (FAA-H-8083-1)

The AMT must change the weight and balance record to indicate the new empty weight and EWCG, and the equipment list is revised to show which equipment is actually installed. The AFM/POH for each individual aircraft includes an aircraft specific equipment list of the items from this master list. When any item is added to or removed from the aircraft, its weight and arm are determined in the equipment list and used to update the weight and balance record.

9. What length of time can an aircraft be flown with inoperative equipment on board? (AC 91-67)

An operator may defer maintenance on inoperative equipment that has been deactivated or removed and placarded inoperative. When the aircraft is due for inspection in accordance with the regulation, the operator should have all inoperative items repaired or replaced. If an owner does not want specific inoperative equipment repaired, then the maintenance person must check each item to see if it conforms to the requirements of 14 CFR §91.213. The maintenance person must ensure that each item of inoperative equipment that is to remain inoperative is placarded appropriately.

10. What regulations apply concerning the operation of an aircraft that has had alterations or repairs which may have substantially affected its operation in flight? (14 CFR 91.407)

No person may operate or carry passengers in any aircraft that has undergone maintenance, preventive maintenance, rebuilding, or alteration that may have appreciably changed its flight characteristics or substantially affected its operation in flight until an appropriately-rated pilot with at least a private pilot certificate

a. flies the aircraft,

b. makes an operational check of the maintenance performed or alteration made, and

c. logs the flight in the aircraft records.

11. How long does the Airworthiness Certificate of an aircraft remain valid? (14 CFR Part 21)

Standard Airworthiness Certificates are effective as long as the maintenance, preventive maintenance, and alterations are performed in accordance with Parts 43 and 91 and the aircraft is registered in the United States.

12. What are the required maintenance inspections for aircraft? (14 CFR 91.409)

a. Annual inspection—within the preceding 12 calendar months.

b. 100-hour inspection—if carrying any person (other than a crewmember) for hire or giving flight instruction for hire.

Note: If an aircraft is operated for hire, it must have a 100-hour inspection as well as an annual inspection when due. If not operated for hire, it must have an annual inspection only.

13. Can a 100-hour inspection be substituted for an annual inspection? (14 CFR 91.409)

No, an annual inspection is acceptable as a 100-hour inspection, but the reverse is not true. The 100-hour inspection is generally the same as an annual inspection but is not considered as intense an inspection as the annual. Also, the 100-hour inspection can be signed off by an Airframe and Powerplant Mechanic (A&P), but the annual inspection must be signed off by an Inspection Authorization (IA) Certificate holder.

14. What types of aircraft inspections can be substituted for a 100-hour inspection? (14 CFR 91.409)

The following may replace a 100-hour inspection:

a. Aircraft inspected in accordance with an approved aircraft inspection program under Part 125 or 135.

b. Progressive inspections which provide for the complete inspection of an aircraft by specifying the intervals in hours and days when routine and detailed inspections will be performed during a 12-calendar month period.

c. Inspection programs approved by the Administrator for large aircraft, turbojet multi-engine airplanes, turboprop-powered multi-engine airplanes and turbine powered rotorcraft.

15. If an aircraft, carrying passengers for hire, has been on a schedule of inspection every 100 hours, under what condition may it continue to operate beyond the 100 hours without a new inspection? (14 CFR 91.409)

The 100-hour limitation may be exceeded by not more than 10 hours while en route to reach a place where the inspection can be done. The excess time used to reach a place where the inspection can be done must be included in computing the next 100 hours of time in service.

16. What are the required tests and inspections of aircraft and equipment to be legal for both VFR and IFR flights? (14 CFR 91.171, 91.207, 91.409, 91.411, 91.413)

a. The aircraft must have an annual inspection. If carrying any person (other than a crewmember) for hire or giving flight instruction for hire, it must also have a 100-hour inspection. A record must be kept in the aircraft/engine logbooks.

b. The static pressure system must be checked within the preceding 24 calendar months. A record must be kept in the aircraft logbook. (IFR requirement)

c. The transponder must have been checked within the preceding 24 calendar months. A record must be kept in the aircraft logbook.

d. The altimeter must have been checked within the preceding 24 calendar months. A record must be kept in the aircraft logbook. (IFR requirement)

e. The VOR must have been checked within the preceding 30 days. A record must be kept in a bound logbook. (IFR requirement)

f. If operations require an emergency locator transmitter (ELT), it must be inspected within 12 calendar months after the last inspection.

Note: Be capable of locating the last 100-hour/annual inspections in the aircraft and engine logbooks and be able to determine when the next inspections are due. Also, be capable of locating all required inspections for instruments and equipment necessary for legal VFR/IFR flight.

17. Define preventive maintenance. (FAA-H-8083-25)

Preventive maintenance is considered to be simple or minor preservation operations and the replacement of small standard parts not involving complex assembly operations. Certificated pilots, excluding student pilots, sport pilots, and recreational pilots, may perform preventive maintenance on any aircraft that is owned or operated by them provided that aircraft is not used in air carrier service. 14 CFR Part 43 identifies typical preventive maintenance operations which include such basic items as oil changes, wheel bearing lubrication, hydraulic fluid (brakes, landing gear system) refills.

18. What are Airworthiness Directives? (FAA-H-8083-25)

An "AD" is the medium used by the FAA to notify aircraft owners and other potentially interested persons of unsafe conditions that may exist because of design defects, maintenance, or other causes, and to specify the conditions under which the product may continue to be operated. They are either of an emergency nature requiring immediate compliance upon receipt, or a less urgent nature requiring compliance within a longer period of time. ADs are regulatory and compliance is mandatory, unless specific exemption is granted.

19. Who is responsible for ensuring that all ADs have been complied with? (FAA-H-8083-25)

It is the aircraft owner or operator's responsibility to assure compliance with all pertinent ADs. 14 CFR requires that a record be maintained showing the current status of applicable ADs, including the method of compliance, and the signature and certificate number of the repair station or mechanic who performed the work.

Additional Study Questions

1. As a newly-certificated commercial pilot, you are ready to use your certificate. Can you begin charging for your services? (AC 120-12)

2. As a commercial pilot, being paid for your services, what Federal Aviation Regulations must you comply with?

3. To act as pilot-in-command of an aircraft during IFR operations under Part 135, what minimum experience is required?

4. Does an aircraft registration certificate have an expiration date? (14 CFR Part 47)

5. What length of time is a temporary registration certificate valid? (14 CFR Part 47)

6. Where can a pilot find the applicable Airworthiness Directives that must be complied with for a specific airplane? (FAA-H-8083-25)

7. How can a pilot determine if all Airworthiness Directives have been complied with for a particular airplane? (FAA-H-8083-25)

8. Aircraft maintenance records must include what information? (14 CFR 91.417)

9. Are Minimum Equipment Lists available for all aircraft? (AC 91-67)

10. How can a pilot determine which placards are required to be displayed in a particular airplane? (POH/AFM)

Weather $\quad$ **2**

A. Weather Briefing Services

1. What is the primary means of obtaining a weather briefing? (AIM 7-1-2)

The primary source of preflight weather briefings is an individual briefing obtained from a briefer at the AFSS/FSS. These briefings, which are tailored to your specific flight, are available 24 hours a day through the use of the toll-free number (1-800-WX BRIEF).

2. What are some examples of other sources of weather information? (AIM 7-1-2)

a. Telephone Information Briefing Service (TIBS) (AFSS)

b. In Alaska, Transcribed Weather Broadcast (TWEB) and telephone access to TWEB (TEL-TWEB).

c. Weather and aeronautical information from numerous private industry sources.

d. The Direct User Access Terminal System (DUATS)

3. Where can you find a listing of FSS and weather information numbers? (AIM 7-1-2)

Numbers for these services can be found in the Airport/Facility Directory under "FAA and NWS Telephone Numbers" section. They are also listed in the U.S. Government section of the local telephone directory.

4. What type of weather briefings are available from an FSS briefer? (AIM 7-1-4)

Standard Briefing—Request anytime you are planning a flight and you have not received a previous briefing or have not received preliminary information through mass-dissemination media; e.g., TIBS, TWEB, etc.

Abbreviated Briefing—Request when you need information to supplement mass-disseminated data, update a previous briefing, or when you need only one or two items.

Continued...

Outlook Briefing— Request whenever your proposed time of departure is six or more hours from the time of the briefing. This is for planning purposes only.

Inflight Briefing—Request when needed to update a preflight briefing.

5. What pertinent information should a weather briefing include? (AIM 7-1-4)

a. Adverse Conditions

b. VFR Flight Not Recommended

c. Synopsis

d. Current Conditions

e. Enroute Forecast

f. Destination Forecast

g. Winds Aloft

h. Notices to Airmen

i. ATC Delay

j. Pilots may obtain the following from AFSS/FSS briefers upon request: Information on Special Use Airspace (Alert Areas, MOAs, Prohibited Areas, Restricted Areas, Military Training Routes, etc.), a review of printed NOTAMs, approximate density altitude information, information on air traffic services and rules, customs/immigration procedures, ADIZ rules, search and rescue, LORAN-C NOTAMs, GPS RAIM availability, and other assistance as required.

6. What is EFAS? (AIM 7-1-5)

Enroute Flight Advisory Service is specifically designed to provide enroute aircraft with timely and meaningful weather advisories pertinent to the type of flight intended, route of flight, and altitude. EFAS is also a central collection and distribution point for pilot-reported weather information (PIREPs). EFAS provides communications capabilities for aircraft flying at 5,000 feet AGL to 17,500 feet MSL on a common frequency of 122.0 MHz. Also known as "Flight Watch."

7. What is HIWAS? (AIM 7-1-10)

Hazardous In-flight Weather Advisory Service is a continuous broadcast of inflight weather advisories including summarized Aviation Weather Warnings, SIGMETs, Convective SIGMETs, Center Weather Advisories, AIRMETs, and urgent PIREPs. HIWAS is an additional source of hazardous weather information which makes this data available on a continuous basis. NAVAIDs with HIWAS capability are depicted on sectionals by an "H" in the upper right corner of the identification box.

8. What is ATIS? (AIM 4-1-13)

Automatic Terminal Information Service — the continuous broadcast of recorded noncontrol information in selected high activity terminal areas. Its purpose is to improve controller effectiveness and to relieve frequency congestion by automating the repetitive transmission of essential but routine information. The information is continuously broadcast over a discrete VHF radio frequency or the voice portion of a local NAVAID, and updated upon the receipt of any official hourly and special weather.

9. What type of information is provided in an ATIS broadcast? (AIM 4-1-13)

Information includes the time of the latest weather sequence, ceiling, visibility, obstructions to visibility, temperature, dew point (if available), wind direction (magnetic), and velocity, altimeter, other pertinent remarks, instrument approach and runway in use.

B. Weather Reports and Forecasts

1. What is a METAR? (AC 00-45)

A METAR is an aviation routine weather report; a weather observer's interpretation of the weather conditions at a given site and time. METARs contain the following elements in this order: Type of report, ICAO station identifier, date and time of report, modifier (as required), wind, visibility, runway visual range (RVR) (as required), weather phenomena, sky condition, temperature/dew point group, altimeter and remarks (RMK) (as required).

Example:
METAR KLAX 140651Z AUTO 00000KT 1SM
R35L/4500V6000FT -RA BR BKN030 10/10 A2990 RMK AO2

2. Describe the various types of weather observing programs now in use. (AIM 7-1-12)

Manual observations—Reports made from airport locations staffed by FAA or NWS personnel.

AWOS—Automated Weather Observing System; consists of various sensors, a processor, a computer-generated voice subsystem, and a transmitter to broadcast local, minute-by-minute weather data directly to the pilot. Observations will include the prefix AUTO in data.

AWOS broadcasts—In addition to the AWOS computer-generated voice, some systems are configured to permit station personnel to append the automated report with an operator-generated message.

ASOS/AWSS—Automated Surface Observing System (ASOS)/ Automated Weather Sensor System (AWSS), the primary surface weather observing system of the U.S. Provides the continuous minute-by-minute observations necessary to generate METARs and other aviation weather information. The information may be transmitted over a discrete VHF radio frequency or the voice portion of a local NAVAID.

3. What are PIREPs and where are they usually found?
(AC 00-45)

These reports contain information concerning weather as observed by pilots en route. Required elements for all PIREPs are message type, location, time (in UTC), flight level (altitudes are MSL), type of aircraft, and at least one weather element encountered (visibility in SM, distances in NM). A PIREP (abbreviation for "pilot reports") is usually transmitted as an individual report but can be appended to a surface aviation weather report or placed into collectives. Also referred to in coded reports as "UA."

4. What are Radar Weather Reports (SD)? (AC 00-45)

These include the type, intensity, and location of the echo top of general areas of precipitation observed by radar, reported each hour at H+35. All heights are reported above MSL. SDs should be used along with METARs, satellite photos, and forecasts when planning a flight to help in thunderstorm area avoidance; once airborne, pilots should depend on Flight Watch.

5. What are Terminal Aerodrome Forecasts (TAFs)?
(AC 00-45)

A TAF is a concise statement of the expected meteorological conditions within a 5 SM radius from the center of an airport's runway complex during a 24-hour time period. TAFs use the same code as METAR in the following format: Type (routine or amended), ICAO station identifier, date and time of origin, valid period date and time, and forecasts. Issued four times daily and valid for 24 hours.

Note: Effective November 5, 2008, the NWS changed the TAF date and time format to conform to international standards outlined in ICAO Annex 3. The change includes the initiating of 30-hour TAFs for 32 high-impact U.S. airports. The remainder of TAF reporting stations will continue with 24-hour forecasts. The date and time format of all TAFs has changed to accommodate the extended TAF period.

a. Valid time changes to *ddhh/ddhh* (from current *ddhhhh*).

b. TEMPOs and PROBs groups change to *ddhh/ddhh* (from current *hhhh*).

c. FROM groups change to *ddhhmm* (from current *hhmm*).

6. What is an Aviation Area Forecast (FA)? (AC 00-45)

An FA is a forecast of VMC, clouds, and general weather conditions over an area the size of several states. It is used to determine forecast enroute weather and to interpolate conditions at airports which do not issue TAFs. FAs are issued three times a day by the Aviation Weather Center (AWC) for each of the 6 areas in the contiguous 48 states. The weather forecast office in Honolulu issues FAs for Hawaii. The Alaska Aviation Weather Unit in Anchorage produces the FA for the entire state of Alaska.

7. What are Inflight Aviation Weather Advisories (WST, WS, WA)? (AC 00-45)

Inflight Aviation Weather Advisories are forecasts to advise en route aircraft of development of potentially hazardous weather. All heights are referenced to MSL, except in the case of ceilings (CIG) which indicates above ground level. The advisories are of three types: Convective SIGMET (WST), SIGMET (WS), and AIRMET (WA).

8. What is a convective SIGMET? (AC 00-45)

Convective SIGMETs (WST) imply severe or greater turbulence, severe icing and low-level wind shear. They may be issued for any convective situation which the forecaster feels is hazardous to all categories of aircraft. Bulletins are issued hourly at H+55, and special bulletins are issued at any time as required and updated at H+55. The text of the bulletin consists of either an observation and a forecast, or just a forecast (valid for up to 2 hours):

a. Severe thunderstorms due to:
   • Surface winds greater than or equal to 50 knots.
   • Hail at the surface greater than or equal to $\frac{3}{4}$ inches in diameter.
   • Tornadoes.

b. Embedded thunderstorms.

c. A line of thunderstorms.

d. Thunderstorms that produce precipitation levels greater than or equal to heavy-intensity precipitation, affecting 40% or more of an area at least 3,000 square miles.

9. What is a SIGMET (WS)? (AC 00-45)

A SIGMET (WS) advises of non-convective weather that is potentially hazardous to all aircraft. SIGMETs are issued for the six areas corresponding to the FA areas. The maximum forecast period is four hours. In the conterminous U.S., SIGMETs are issued when the following phenomena occur or are expected to occur:

a. Severe icing not associated with a thunderstorm.

b. Severe or extreme turbulence or clear air turbulence (CAT) not associated with thunderstorms.

c. Duststorms or sandstorms lowering surface or inflight visibilities to below 3 miles.

d. Volcanic ash.

10. What is an AIRMET (WA)? (AC 00-45)

An AIRMET is an advisory of significant weather phenomena for conditions at intensities lower than required for issuance of SIGMETs, issued every 6 hours beginning at 0145 UTC (central daylight time). Pilots should use AIRMETs in the preflight and enroute phase of flight to enhance safety. Each AIRMET bulletin includes an outlook for conditions expected after the valid period, and contain details about IFR, extensive mountain obscuration, turbulence, strong surface winds, icing, and freezing levels.

11. What are the different types of AIRMETs? (AIM 7-1-6)

There are three types of AIRMETs, Sierra, Tango, and Zulu:

a. AIRMET Sierra describes IFR conditions and/or extensive mountain obscurations.

b. AIRMET Tango describes moderate turbulence, sustained surface winds of 30 knots or greater, and/or nonconvective low-level wind shear.

c. AIRMET Zulu describes moderate icing and provides freezing level heights.

12. What is a winds and temperatures aloft forecast (FB)? (AC 00-45)

Winds and temperatures aloft are forecast for specific locations in the contiguous U.S. and also for a network of locations in Alaska and Hawaii. These forecasts, called FBs, are issued 4 times daily. In an FB, a 4-digit code group shows wind direction, in reference to true north, and wind speed in knots, with an additional 2-digit code group showing forecast temperatures in degrees Celsius.

13. What valuable information can be determined from an FB? (AC 00-45)

Most favorable altitude—based on winds and direction of flight.

Areas of possible icing—by noting air temperatures of +2°C to -20°C.

Temperature inversions.

Turbulence—by observing abrupt changes in wind direction and speed at different altitudes.

14. What is a Center Weather Advisory (CWA)? (AC 00-45)

Issued by a CWSU (Center Weather Service Unit), this is an aviation warning for use by aircrews to anticipate and avoid adverse weather conditions in the enroute and terminal environments. The CWA is a short-term "nowcast," pinpointing hazardous weather already causing an impact or expected to cause an impact within a 2-hour period; therefore it is an inflight advisory rather than a flight planning tool. CWAs are valid for a maximum of 2 hours; if conditions are expected to continue beyond the 2-hour valid period, a statement will be included in the CWA.

15. What is a Convective Outlook (AC)? (AC 00-45)

The AC is a flight planning tool used to avoid thunderstorms, issued in Day 1 and Day 2 time-period parts, which describes the prospects for general thunderstorm activity during the following 24-hour periods. Areas in which there is high, moderate, or slight risk of severe thunderstorms are included as well as areas where thunderstorms may approach severe limits.

C. Aviation Weather Charts

1. What is a surface analysis chart? (AC 00-45)

This is a computer-prepared chart transmitted every three hours that covers the contiguous 48 states and adjacent areas. Provides a ready means of locating pressure systems and fronts. It also gives an overview of winds, temperatures and dew point temperatures at chart time. Since weather moves and conditions change, using the surface analysis chart along with other weather information gives a more complete weather picture.

2. What is a radar summary chart? (AC 00-45)

This is a computer-generated graphical display of a collection of automated radar weather reports, available hourly with a valid time of 35 minutes past each hour. Displays areas of precipitation as well as information about type, intensity, configuration, coverage, echo top, and cell movement of precipitation (and severe weather watches, if in effect when the chart is valid). It aids in preflight planning by identifying general areas and movement of precipitation and/or thunderstorms; however, it displays drops or ice particles of precipitation size only — it does not display clouds and fog. Therefore, since the absence of echoes does not guarantee clear weather, and cloud tops will most likely be higher than the tops of the precipitation echoes detected by radar, the radar summary chart must be used along with other charts, reports, and forecasts for best effectiveness.

3. What is a winds and temperature aloft chart? (AC 00-45)

This chart is computer-generated from FB (previously called FD) reports, depicting both observed and forecast winds and temperatures aloft. Forecast winds and temperatures aloft are prepared for eight levels on eight separate panels: 6,000, 9,000, 12,000, 18,000, 24,000, 30,000, 34,000 and 39,000 feet MSL. They are available daily as 12-hour progs valid at 1200Z and 0000Z. FB charts are typically used to determine winds at a proposed altitude or to select the best altitude for a proposed flight; also, temperatures can be determined from the forecast charts. Interpolation must be used to determine winds and temperatures at a level between charts and data when the time period is other than the valid time on the chart.

4. What are significant weather prognostic charts?
(AC 00-45)

These "prog" charts portray forecasts of selected weather conditions at specified valid times (12, 24, 36, and 48 hour). Each valid time is the time at which the forecast conditions are expected to occur, made from a comprehensive set of observed weather conditions. The observed conditions are extended forward in time and become forecasts by considering atmospheric and environmental processes. For forecast information for the surface to 24,000 feet, use the low-level significant weather prog chart, and for above 24,000 to 60,000 feet, use the high-level significant weather prog chart.

5. What is a convective outlook chart? (AC 00-45)

This chart depicts areas forecast to have the potential for severe (tornado, wind gusts 50 knots or greater, or hail $\frac{3}{4}$-inch diameter size or greater) and non-severe (general) convection and specific severe weather threats during the following three days. The chart defines areas of slight risk (SLGT), moderate risk (MDT) or high risk (HIGH) of severe thunderstorms for a 24-hour period beginning at 1200 UTC. The Day 1 and Day 2 Convective Outlooks also depict areas of general thunderstorms (GEN TSTMS), while the Day 1, Day 2, and Day 3 Convective Outlooks may use SEE TEXT for areas where convection may approach or slightly exceed severe criteria.

D. NOTAMs

1. What are NOTAMs? (AIM 5-1-3)

Notices To Airmen (NOTAM)—Time critical aeronautical information which is of either a temporary nature or not sufficiently known in advance to permit publication on aeronautical charts or in other operational publications receives immediate dissemination via the National NOTAM System. It includes such information as airport or primary runway closures, changes in the status of navigational aids, ILS's, radar service availability, and other information essential to planned enroute, terminal, or landing operations.

2. What are the four basic groups of NOTAMs?
(Order 7930.2)

NOTAMs are classified into four groups:

a. *(D) NOTAMs*—Information that requires wide dissemination via telecommunication and pertains to en route navigational aids, civil public-use airports listed in the AFD, facilities, services, and procedures.

b. *FDC NOTAMs*—Flight information that is regulatory in nature including, but not limited to, changes to IFR charts, procedures, and airspace usage.

c. *POINTER NOTAMs*—Issued by a flight service station to high-light or point out another NOTAM; such as an FDC NOTAM. These NOTAMs assist users in cross-referencing important information that may not be found under an airport or NAVAID identifier.

d. *MILITARY NOTAMs*—Pertain to U.S. Air Force, Army, Marine, and Navy navigational aids/airports that are part of the NAS.

3. All (D) NOTAMs will have keywords contained within the first part of the text. What are several examples of these keywords? (Order 7930.2)

RWY	TWY	RAMP	APRON	AD
OBST	NAV	COM	SVC	AIRSPACE

U (unverified movement area)
O (other aeronautical information)

4. Where can NOTAM information be obtained? (AIM 5-1-3)

a. Nearest FSS

b. DUATS vendors

c. NTAP printed NOTAMs. Not normally provided in a briefing so pilots must make specific request for them during briefing. The NTAP is also available online at the FAA website.

E. Aviation Weather Hazards

1. What are the two major classifications of thunderstorms? (AC 00-6)

Air mass thunderstorms — Most often result from surface heating. They occur at random in unstable air and last for only an hour or two. They reach maximum intensity and frequency over land during middle and late afternoon. Off-shore they reach a maximum during late hours of darkness when land temperature is coolest and cool air flows off the land over the relatively warm water.

Steady-state thunderstorms — Usually form in lines, last for several hours, dump heavy rain and possibly hail, and produce strong gusty winds and possibly tornadoes. They are normally associated with weather systems. Fronts, converging winds, and troughs aloft force upward motion spawning these storms which often form into squall lines. They are intensified by afternoon heating.

2. What procedures should be followed when avoiding turbulence around thunderstorms? (AIM 7-1-29)

Never regard any thunderstorm lightly even when radar observers report the echoes are of light intensity. Avoiding thunderstorms is the best policy, but these are some "do's and don'ts":

a. Don't land or take off in the face of an approaching thunderstorm. A sudden gust front of low-level turbulence could cause loss of control.

b. Don't attempt to fly under a thunderstorm even if you can see through to the other side. Turbulence and wind shear under the storm could be disastrous.

c. Don't fly without airborne radar into a cloud mass containing scattered embedded thunderstorms. Scattered thunderstorms not embedded can usually be visually circumnavigated.

d. Don't trust the visual appearance to be a reliable indicator of the turbulence inside a thunderstorm.

e. Do avoid, by at least 20 miles, any thunderstorms identified as severe or giving an intense radar echo. This is especially true under the anvil of a large cumulonimbus cloud.

f. Do clear the top of a known or suspected severe thunderstorm by at least 1,000 feet altitude for each 10 knots of wind speed at the cloud top. (*Note:* This should exceed the altitude capability of most aircraft.)

g. Do circumnavigate the entire area if the area has 6/10 thunderstorm coverage.

h. Do remember that vivid and frequent lightning indicates the probability of a severe thunderstorm.

i. Do regard as extremely hazardous any thunderstorm with tops of 35,000 feet or higher whether the top is visually sighted or determined by radar.

3. Can ATC provide inflight assistance in avoiding thunderstorms and severe weather? (AIM 7-1-14)

Yes, to the extent possible, controllers will issue pertinent information on weather or chaff areas and assist pilots in avoiding such areas when requested. Pilots should respond to a weather advisory by either acknowledging the advisory or by requesting an alternate course of action as appropriate.

However, the controller's primary responsibility is to provide safe separation between aircraft. Additional services such as weather avoidance assistance can only be provided to the extent that it doesn't interfere with their primary function. ATC radar limitations and frequency congestion may also limit the controller's capability to assist.

4. Give some examples of charts and reports useful in determining the potential for and location of thunderstorms along your route. (AC 00-45)

a. A *convective outlook* (AC) describes the prospects for general thunderstorm activity during the following 24 hours. Areas in which there is a high, moderate, or slight risk of severe thunderstorms are included, as well as areas where thunderstorms may approach severe limits.

b. A *composite moisture stability chart* outlines areas of stable/unstable air, moisture, and possible aviation hazards.

c. A *radar summary chart* graphically displays a collection of radar reports. The chart displays the type of precipitation

Continued...

echoes and indicates their intensity, intensity trend, configuration, coverage, echo tops and bases, and movement.

d. A *convective outlook chart* depicts areas of probable thunderstorm activity.

e. *Pilot Reports* (PIREPs) help in determining the actual conditions along your planned route of flight.

5. What are microbursts? (AIM 7-1-26)

Microbursts are small-scale intense downdrafts which, on reaching the surface, spread outward in all directions from the downdraft center. This causes the presence of both vertical and horizontal wind shears that can be extremely hazardous to all types and categories of aircraft, especially at low altitudes. Due to their small size, short life span, and the fact that they can occur over areas without surface precipitation, microbursts are not easily detectable using conventional weather radar or wind shear alert systems.

6. Where are microbursts most likely to occur? (AIM 7-1-26)

Microbursts can be found almost anywhere there is convective activity. They may be embedded in heavy rain associated with a thunderstorm or in light rain in benign-appearing virga. When there is little or no precipitation at the surface accompanying the microburst, a ring of blowing dust may be the only visual clue of its existence.

7. What are some basic characteristics of a microburst? (AIM 7-1-26)

Size: less than 1 mile in diameter as it descends from the cloud base; can extend $2\frac{1}{2}$ miles in diameter near ground level.

Intensity: downdrafts as strong as 6,000 feet per minute; horizontal winds near the surface can be as strong as 45 knots resulting in a 90-knot wind shear (headwind to tailwind change for traversing aircraft).

Duration: an individual microburst will seldom last longer than 15 minutes from the time it strikes the ground until dissipation. Sometimes microbursts are concentrated into a line structure, and under these conditions activity may continue for as long as an hour.

8. How can microburst encounters be avoided? (AC 00-54)

The following should be examined for clues of potential microburst/windshear conditions affecting the flight:

TAFs—examine the terminal forecast for convective activity.

METARs—inspect for windshear clues (thunderstorms, rainshowers, blowing dust).

Severe weather watch reports—check for issuance since severe convective weather is a prime source for microwbursts.

LLWAS reports—Low Level Windshear Alert System, designed to detect wind shifts between outlying stations and a reference station.

SIGMETs and convective SIGMETs—may provide essential clues.

Visual clues from the cockpit—heavy rain (in a dry or moist environment) which can be accompanied by curling outflow, a ring of blowing dust or localized dust in general, flying debris, virga, a rain core with rain diverging away horizontally from the rain core, or tornadic features (funnel clouds, tornadoes). At night, lightning may be the only visual clue.

PIREPs—reports of sudden airspeed changes in the airport approach or landing corridors provide indication of the presence of windshear.

Airborne weather radar—to detect convective cells.

9. Define wind shear and state the areas in which it is likely to occur. (AC 00-54)

Wind shear is the rate of change of wind velocity (direction and/or speed) per unit distance; conventionally expressed as vertical or horizontal wind shear. It may occur at any level in the atmosphere but three areas are of special concern:

a. Wind shear with a low-level temperature inversion;

b. Wind shear in a frontal zone or thunderstorm; and

c. Clear air turbulence (CAT) at high levels associated with a jet stream or strong circulation.

10. Why is wind shear an operational concern to pilots? (AC 00-6)

Wind shear is an operational concern because unexpected changes in wind speed and direction can be potentially very hazardous to aircraft operations at low altitudes on approach to and departing from airports.

11. What airplane characteristics will be observed in the following wind shear situations?
— a sudden increase in headwind.
— a sudden decrease in headwind.

Increased headwind—As a tailwind shears to a constant headwind, an increase in airspeed and altitude occurs along with a nose-up pitching tendency. The usual reaction is to reduce both power and pitch. This reaction can be dangerous if the aircraft suddenly encounters a downdraft and tailwind. Now the situation demands the exact opposite of the pilot's initial reaction: a need for more performance from the airplane instead of less (more power/increased pitch attitude).

Decreased headwind—As a headwind shears to a calm or tailwind, pitch attitude decreases, airspeed decreases, and a loss of altitude occurs. The required action is more power and higher pitch attitude to continue a climb or remain on the glide slope.

12. Concerning wind shear detection, what does the abbreviation LLWAS indicate? (AIM 4-3-7)

Low-Level Wind Shear Alert System (LLWAS) is a computerized system that detects the presence of a possible hazardous low-level wind shear by continuously comparing the winds measured by sensors installed around the periphery of an airport with the wind measured at the center of the airport. If the difference between the center field wind sensor and a peripheral wind sensor becomes excessive, a thunderstorm or thunderstorm gust front wind shear is possible.

Additional Study Questions

1. When the ceiling/sky, visibility, and obstructions to vision are omitted in the ATIS, what condition is indicated? (AC 00-45)

2. How can a pilot receive updated weather information inflight? (AIM 7-1-5)

3. Briefly describe the type of information provided by the different aviation weather charts. (AC 00-45)

4. Define the acronyms IFR, MVFR, and VFR. (AC 00-45)

5. Define the term "ceiling." (AC 00-45)

6. From which primary source should information be obtained regarding expected weather at the ETA if your destination has no TAF? (AC 00-45)

7. If the temperature is +16° Centigrade at an elevation of 1,600 feet and a standard (average) temperature lapse rate exists, what will the approximate freezing level be? (AC 00-6)

8. What are the three stages of thunderstorm development? (AC 00-6)

9. What is an occlusion? (AC 00-6)

10. What information will you provide when giving a wind shear report? (AIM 7-1-24)

Airplane
Systems

3

Some of the following questions are in reference to the systems of a Cessna 172-RG. For accuracy, a review of your aircraft's Pilot Operating Handbook should be made.

A. Primary Flight Controls and Trim

1. How are the various flight controls operated?

The flight control surfaces are manually actuated through use of either a rod or cable system. A control wheel actuates the ailerons and elevator, and rudder/brake pedals actuate the rudder.

2. What type of trim system is installed in this airplane?

Both rudder and elevator trim are provided. They are both manually actuated.

B. Wing Flaps, Leading Edge Devices, and Spoilers

1. What are flaps, and what is their function?
(FAA-H-8083-3)

The wing flaps are movable panels on the inboard trailing edges of the wings. They are hinged so they may be extended downward into the flow of air beneath the wings to increase both lift and drag. Their purpose is to permit a slower airspeed and a steeper angle of descent during a landing approach. In some cases, they may also be used to shorten the takeoff distance.

2. Describe a typical wing flap system.

The wing flap system consists of "single-slot" type wing flaps. They are extended and retracted by a wing flap switch lever to flap settings of 10, 20, and 30 degrees. A 15-amp push-to-reset circuit breaker protects the wing flap system circuit.

3. State some examples of leading edge lift devices.
(AC 65-15A)

Slots—A slot in the leading edge of a wing directs high-energy air from under the wing to the airflow above the wing, accelerating upper airflow. By accelerating the airflow above the wing, airflow separation will be delayed to higher angles of attack. This allows the wing to continue to develop lift at substantially higher angles of attack.

Slats—A miniature airfoil mounted on the leading edge of a wing. They may be movable or fixed. At low angles of attack, movable slats are held flush against the leading edge by positive air pressure. At high angles of attack, the slats are moved forward either by the pilot or automatically by the low pressures present at the leading edge. Slats provide the same results as slots.

4. What are spoilers? (AC 65-15A)

Spoilers are devices located on the upper surface of a wing which are designed to reduce lift by "spoiling" the airflow above the wing. They are typically used as speed brakes to slow an airplane down, both in flight as well as on the ground immediately after touchdown.

C. Pitot / Static Flight Instruments

1. What instruments operate from the pitot/static system?
(FAA-H-8083-15)

The pitot/static system operates the altimeter, vertical speed indicator, and airspeed indicator.

2. Does this aircraft have an alternate static air system?

Yes. In the event of external static port blockage, a static pressure alternate source valve is installed. The control is located beneath the throttle, and if used will supply static pressure from inside the cabin, instead of from the external static ports.

3. How does an altimeter work? (FAA-H-8083-15)

Aneroid wafers in the instrument expand and contract as atmospheric pressure changes, and through a shaft and gear linkage, rotate pointers on the dial of the instrument.

4. A pressure altimeter is subject to what limitations? (FAA-H-8083-15)

Non-standard pressure and temperature:

a. Temperature variations expand or contract the atmosphere and raise or lower pressure levels that the altimeter senses.

On a warm day—The pressure level is higher than on a standard day. The altimeter indicates lower than actual altitude.

On a cold day—The pressure level is lower than on a standard day. The altimeter indicates higher than actual altitude.

b. Changes in surface pressure also affect pressure levels at altitude.

Higher than standard pressure—The pressure level is higher than on a standard day. The altimeter indicates lower than actual altitude.

Lower than standard pressure—The pressure level is lower than on a standard day. The altimeter indicates higher than actual altitude.

Remember: High to low or hot to cold, look out below!

5. Define and state how you would determine the following altitudes. (FAA-H-8083-25)

Indicated altitude—the altitude read directly from the altimeter (uncorrected) after it is set to the current altimeter setting.

Pressure altitude—the altitude when the altimeter setting window is adjusted to 29.92. Pressure altitude is used for computer solutions to determine density altitude, true altitude, true airspeed.

True altitude—the true vertical distance of the aircraft above sea level. Airport, terrain, and obstacle elevations found on aeronautical charts are true altitudes.

Density altitude—pressure altitude corrected for nonstandard temperature variations. Directly related to an aircraft's takeoff, climb, and landing performance.

Absolute altitude—the vertical distance of an aircraft above the terrain.

6. How does the airspeed indicator operate?
(FAA-H-8083-25)

It measures the difference between the impact pressure from the pitot head and atmospheric pressure from the static source.

7. What are the limitations of the airspeed indicator?
(FAA-H-8083-25)

The airspeed indicator is subject to proper flow of air in the pitot/static system.

8. The airspeed indicator is subject to what errors?

Position error— Caused by the static ports sensing erroneous static pressure; slipstream flow causes disturbances at the static port, preventing actual atmospheric pressure measurement. It varies with airspeed, altitude, and configuration, and may be a plus or minus value.

Density error— Changes in altitude and temperature are not compensated for by the instrument.

Compressibility error— Caused by the packing of air into the pitot tube at high airspeeds, resulting in higher than normal indications. It is usually not a factor.

9. What are the different types of aircraft speeds?
(FAA-H-8083-25)

True Airspeed (TAS)—The speed of the airplane in relation to the air mass in which it is flying.

Indicated Airspeed (IAS)—The speed of the airplane as observed on the airspeed indicator. It is the airspeed without correction for indicator, position (or installation), or compressibility errors.

Calibrated Airspeed (CAS)—The airspeed indicator reading corrected for position (or installation), and instrument errors. (CAS is equal to TAS at sea level in standard atmosphere.) The color-coding for various design speeds marked on airspeed indicators may be IAS or CAS.

Equivalent Airspeed (EAS)—The airspeed indicator reading corrected for position (or installation), or instrument error, and for adiabatic compressible flow for the particular altitude. (EAS is equal to CAS at sea level in standard atmosphere.)

10. What airspeed limitations apply to the color-coded marking system of the airspeed indicator? (FAA-H-8083-25)

white arc.. flap operating range

lower A/S limit white arc................ V_{S0} (stalling speed or minimum steady flight speed in landing configuration)

upper A/S limit white arc................ V_{FE} (maximum flap extension speed)

green arc.. normal operating range

lower A/S limit green arc................ V_{S1} (stall speed clean or specified configuration)

upper A/S limit green arc................ V_{NO} (normal operations speed or maximum structural cruise speed)

yellow arc .... caution range (operations in smooth air only)

red line .... V_{NE} (maximum speed for operations in smooth air only)

11. What are some examples of important airspeed limitations that are not marked on the face of the airspeed indicator, but are found on placards and in the AFM or POH? (FAA-H-8083-25)

a. Design maneuvering speed (V_A)

b. Landing gear operating speed (V_{LO})

c. Landing gear extended speed (V_{LE})

d. Best angle-of-climb speed (V_X)

e. Best rate-of-climb speed (V_Y)

12. How does the vertical speed indicator work?
(FAA-H-8083-15)

The vertical speed indicator is a pressure differential instrument.
Inside the instrument case is an aneroid very much like the one in
an airspeed indicator. Both the inside of this aneroid and the inside
of the instrument case are vented to the static system, but the case
is vented through a calibrated orifice that causes the pressure inside
the case to change more slowly than the pressure inside the aneroid. As the aircraft ascends, the static pressure becomes lower and
the pressure inside the case compresses the aneroid, moving the
pointer upward, showing a climb and indicating the number of feet
per minute the aircraft is ascending.

13. What are the limitations of the vertical speed indicator?
(FAA-H-8083-25)

It is not accurate until the aircraft is stabilized. Sudden or abrupt
changes in the aircraft attitude will cause erroneous instrument
readings as airflow fluctuates over the static port. Both rough
control technique and turbulent air result in unreliable needle
indications.

D. Gyroscopic Flight Instruments

1. Which instruments contain gyroscopes?
(FAA-H-8083-25)

The most common instruments containing gyroscopes are the turn
coordinator, heading indicator, and attitude indicator.

2. What are the two fundamental properties of a gyroscope? (FAA-H-8083-25)

Rigidity in space—A gyroscope remains in a fixed position in the
plane in which it is spinning.

Precession—The tilting or turning of a gyro in response to a
deflective force. The reaction to this force does not occur at the
point where it was applied; it occurs at a point 90° later in the
direction of rotation. The rate at which the gyro precesses is
inversely proportional to the speed of the rotor and proportional to
the deflective force.

3. What are the various sources that may be used to power the gyroscopic instruments in an airplane? (FAA-H-8083-25)

In some airplanes, all the gyros are vacuum, pressure, or electrically operated; in others, vacuum or pressure systems provide the power for the heading and attitude indicators, while the electrical system provides the power for the turn coordinator. Most airplanes have at least two sources of power to ensure at least one source of bank information if one power source fails.

4. How does the vacuum system operate? (FAA-H-8083-25)

Air is drawn into the vacuum system by the engine-driven vacuum pump. It first goes through a filter, which prevents foreign matter from entering the vacuum or pressure system. The air then moves through the attitude and heading indicators, where it causes the gyros to spin. A relief valve prevents the vacuum pressure, or suction, from exceeding prescribed limits. After that, the air is expelled overboard or used in other systems, such as for inflating pneumatic deicing boots.

5. How does the attitude indicator work? (FAA-H-8083-25)

The attitude indicator's gyro is mounted on a horizontal plane (a bar representing true horizon) and depends upon rigidity in space for its operation. The fixed gyro remains in a horizontal plane as the airplane is pitched or banked about its axis, indicating the attitude of the airplane relative to the true horizon.

6. Discuss the limits of an attitude indicator. (FAA-H-8083-25)

Pitch and bank limits depend upon the make and model of the instrument. Limits in the banking plane are usually from 100°–110°, pitch limits are usually from 60°–70°. If either limit is exceeded, the instrument will tumble or spill giving incorrect indications until reset. Some modern attitude indicators will not tumble.

7. The attitude indicator is subject to what errors?
(FAA-H-8083-15)

Attitude indicators are free from most errors, but depending on the speed with which the erection system functions, there may be a slight nose-up indication during a rapid acceleration and a nose-down indication during a rapid deceleration. There is also a possibility of a small bank angle and pitch error after a 180° turn. These inherent errors are small and correct themselves within a minute or so after returning to straight-and-level flight.

8. How does the heading indicator operate?
(FAA-H-8083-25)

It uses the principle of rigidity in space; the rotor turns in a vertical plane, and the compass card is fixed to the rotor. Since the rotor remains rigid in space, the points on the card hold the same position in space relative to the vertical plane. As the instrument case and the airplane revolve around the vertical axis, the card shows clear, accurate heading information.

9. What are the limitations of the heading indicator?
(FAA-H-8083-25)

Pitch and bank limits vary with design and make of instrument. On some light airplanes, the limits are about 55° of pitch and 55° of bank. When either is exceeded, the instrument "tumbles" or "spills" giving incorrect indications until reset with the caging knob. Some modern instruments are designed in such a manner that they will not tumble.

10. What error is the heading indicator subject to?
(FAA-H-8083-25, FAA-P-8740-16)

Because of precession, caused chiefly by friction, the heading indicator will creep or drift from a heading to which it is set. Among other factors, the amount of drift depends upon the condition of the instrument. The heading indicator may indicate as much as 15 degrees of error per every hour of operation.

11. How does the turn coordinator operate? (FAA-H-8083-25)

The turn part of the instrument uses precession to indicate direction and approximate rate of turn. A gyro reacts by trying to move in reaction to the force applied thus moving the needle or miniature aircraft in proportion to the rate of turn. The slip/skid indicator is a liquid-filled tube with a ball that reacts to centrifugal force and gravity.

12. What information does the turn coordinator provide? (FAA-H-8083-25)

It shows the yaw and roll of the aircraft around the vertical and longitudinal axes. The miniature airplane indicates direction of the turn as well as rate of turn. When aligned with the turn index, it represents a standard rate of turn of 3° per second. The inclinometer of the turn coordinator indicates the coordination of aileron and rudder. The ball indicates whether the airplane is in coordinated flight or is in a slip or skid.

13. What will the turn indicator indicate when the aircraft is in a skidding or a slipping turn? (FAA-H-8083-25)

Skid—The ball in the tube will be to the outside of the turn; too much rate of turn for the amount of bank.

Slip—The ball in the tube will be on the inside of the turn; not enough rate of turn for the amount of bank.

E. Magnetic Compass

1. How does the magnetic compass work? (FAA-H-8083-25)

Magnetized needles fastened to a float assembly, around which is mounted a compass card, align themselves parallel to the earth's lines of magnetic force. The float assembly is housed in a bowl filled with acid-free white kerosene.

2. What limitations does the magnetic compass have? (FAA-H-8083-15)

This jewel-and-pivot type mounting allows the float freedom to rotate and tilt up to approximately 18° angle of bank. At steeper bank angles, the compass indications are erratic and unpredictable.

3. What are the various compass errors? (FAA-H-8083-15)

Oscillation error—Erratic movement of the compass card caused by turbulence or rough control technique.

Deviation error—Due to electrical and magnetic disturbances in the aircraft.

Variation error—Angular difference between true and magnetic north; reference isogonic lines of variation.

Dip errors:
a. *Acceleration error*—On east or west headings, while accelerating, the magnetic compass shows a turn to the north, and when decelerating, it shows a turn to the south.

   Remember: ANDS
   A ccelerate
   N orth
   D ecelerate
   S outh

b. *Northerly turning error*—The compass leads in the south half of a turn, and lags in the north half of a turn.

   Remember: UNOS
   U ndershoot
   N orth
   O vershoot
   S outh

F. Hydraulic System

1. What equipment would be considered hydraulic on this aircraft?

a. The retractable landing gear

b. The emergency hand pump

c. The hydraulically-actuated brake on each main gear

d. The air/oil nose gear shock strut

2. What provides hydraulic power to the landing gear system?

An electrically-driven hydraulic power pack provides all hydraulic power to the landing gear system. The power pack is located behind the firewall between the pilot's and copilot's rudder pedals.

3. Describe hydraulic power pack operation.

Hydraulic power pack operation is controlled by the landing gear lever. When the gear lever is selected in either the "Up" or "Down" position, a pressure switch will activate the power pack and a selector valve is mechanically rotated. Depending on the position of the landing gear lever (and corresponding valve position), hydraulic pressure will be applied in the direction selected. This hydraulic pressure is applied to actuator cylinders, which extend or retract the gear. When the landing gear has reached the desired position and the cycle is complete (a series of electrical switches have closed or opened), an indicator light will illuminate on the panel. In the "Gear Down" cycle only, the hydraulic power pack will continue to operate until system pressure is between 1,000 PSI to 1,500 PSI, at which time the pressure switch turns the power pack off. The hydraulic system normally maintains an operating pressure of 1,000 PSI to 1,500 PSI.

G. Landing Gear

1. Describe the landing gear system on this airplane.

The landing gear consists of a tricycle-type system using two main wheels and a steerable nose wheel. Tubular spring steel main gear struts provide main gear shock absorption, while nose gear shock absorption is provided by a combination air/oil shock strut.

2. How is the landing gear extended and retracted?

A hydraulic actuator powered by an electrically-driven hydraulic power pack enables the landing gear extension, retraction, and main gear down lock release operations to occur. A pressure switch starts and stops power pack operation and hydraulic pressure is directed by a landing gear lever.

3. How is the gear locked in the down position?

Mechanical down locks are incorporated into the nose and main gear assembly.

4. How is the gear locked in the up position?

A positive "up" pressure is maintained on the landing gear by the hydraulic power pack. To accomplish this, the power pack automatically maintains an operating pressure of 1,000 PSI to 1,500 PSI in the landing gear system.

5. How is accidental gear retraction prevented on the ground?

Inadvertent gear retraction is prevented by a safety (squat) switch on the nose gear. Whenever the nose gear strut is compressed (weight of the airplane on the ground), this switch electrically prevents operation of the landing gear system.

6. How is the landing gear position indicated in the cockpit?

Amber (gear up) and green (gear down) position indicator lights are provided in the cockpit. They are located adjacent to the landing gear control lever and indicate that the gear is either up or down and locked. Both indicators incorporate a press-to-test feature and also provide dimming shutters for night operation.

Note: If one of the indicator lights should burn out, the design allows for replacement inflight, with the bulb from the other indicator light.

7. What type of landing gear warning system is used?

If the manifold pressure is reduced to less than approximately 12 inches at a low altitude with the master switch on, and the landing gear is not locked down, a switch on the throttle linkage will electrically actuate the gear warning circuit of the dual warning unit. An intermittent tone will be heard on the speaker. Also, if the wing flaps are extended beyond 20° while the landing gear is in the retracted position, an interconnect switch in the wing flap system will cause the horn to sound.

8. What is the normal length of time necessary for landing gear retraction or extension?

5 to 7 seconds for either extension or retraction of the landing gear.

9. Can the landing gear be retracted with the hand-operated pump?

No, retraction of the landing gear cannot be accomplished with the emergency hand pump.

10. Describe the braking system on this aircraft.

Hydraulically-actuated disc-type brakes are used on each main gear wheel. A hydraulic line connects each brake to a master cylinder located on each pilot's rudder pedals. By applying pressure to the top of either the pilot's or copilot's set of rudder pedals, the brakes may be applied.

11. How is steering accomplished on the ground?
(AC 65-15A)

Light airplanes are generally provided with nosewheel steering capabilities through a simple system of mechanical linkages connected to the rudder pedals. When a rudder pedal is depressed, a spring-loaded bungee (push-pull rod) connected to the pivotal portion of a nosewheel strut will turn the nosewheel.

12. What are the landing gear tire pressures?

Nosewheel Tire Pressure................. 40 – 50 PSI
5.00-5, 6-ply rated tires

Main Wheel Tire Pressure .... 60 – 68 PSI
15x6.00-6, 6-ply rated tires

H. Powerplant

1. What type of engine does this aircraft have?

The airplane is powered by an engine manufactured by Avco-Lycoming, rated at 180 horsepower at 2,700 rpm. It may be described as follows:

a. Normally aspirated

b. Direct-drive

c. Air-cooled

d. Horizontally-opposed

e. Carburetor-equipped

f. Four-cylinder

g. 361-cubic-inch displacement

2. Describe how each of the following engine gauges work.

Oil Temperature—Electrically powered from the aircraft electrical system.

Oil Pressure—A direct-pressure oil line from the engine delivers oil at engine operating pressure to the gauge.

Cylinder Head Temperature—Electrically powered from the aircraft electrical system.

Tachometer—Engine-driven mechanically.

Manifold pressure—Direct reading of induction air manifold pressure in inches of mercury.

Fuel pressure—Indicates fuel pressure to the carburetor.

3. What four strokes must occur in each cylinder of a typical four-stroke engine in order for it to produce full power? (FAA-H-8083-25)

The four strokes are:

Intake —fuel mixture is drawn into cylinder by downward stroke.

Compression—mixture is compressed by upward stroke.

Power—spark ignites mixture forcing piston downward and producing power.

Exhaust—burned gases pushed out of cylinder by upward stroke.

4. What does the carburetor do? (FAA-H-8083-25)

Carburetion may be defined as the process of mixing fuel and air in the correct proportions to form a combustible mixture. The carburetor vaporizes liquid fuel into small particles and then mixes it with air. It measures the airflow and meters fuel accordingly.

5. How does the carburetor heat system work? (AFM)

A carburetor heat valve, controlled by the pilot, allows unfiltered, heated air from a shroud located around an exhaust riser or muffler to be directed to the induction air manifold prior to the carburetor. Carburetor heat should be used anytime suspected or known carburetor icing conditions exist.

6. What is fuel injection? (FAA-H-8083-25)

Fuel injectors have replaced carburetors in some airplanes. In a fuel injection system, the fuel is normally injected into the system either directly into the cylinders or just ahead of the intake valves; whereas in a carbureted system, the fuel enters the airstream at the throttle valve. There are several types of fuel injection systems in use today, and though there are variations in design, the operational methods are generally simple. Most designs incorporate an engine-driven fuel pump, a fuel/control unit, fuel distributor, and discharge nozzle for each cylinder.

7. What are some advantages of fuel injection? (FAA-H-8083-25)

a. Reduction in evaporative icing

b. Better fuel flow

c. Faster throttle response

d. Precise control of mixture

e. Better fuel distribution

f. Easier cold weather starts

8. Are there any disadvantages associated with fuel-injected engines? (FAA-H-8083-25)

a. Difficulty in starting a hot engine

b. Vapor locks during ground operations on hot days

c. Problems associated with restarting an engine that quits because of fuel starvation

9. What is the condition known as vapor lock? (AC 65-12A)

Fuel-injected engines are more susceptible to vapor lock during ground operations on hot days. Vapor lock occurs when fuel vapor and/or air collect in different sections of the fuel system. The fuel may actually boil in the lines, creating a condition which interferes with the normal operation of valves, pumps, etc. Other causes of vapor lock can be low fuel pressure and excessive fuel turbulence.

10. What does the throttle do? (FAA-H-8083-25)

The throttle allows the pilot to manually control the amount of fuel/air charge entering the cylinders. This in turn regulates the engine manifold pressure.

11. What does the mixture control do? (FAA-H-8083-25)

It regulates the fuel-to-air ratio. Most airplane engines incorporate a device called a mixture control, by which the fuel/air ratio can be controlled by the pilot during flight. The purpose of a mixture control is to prevent the mixture from becoming too rich at high altitudes, due to decreasing air density. Leaning the mixture during cross-country flights conserves fuel and provides optimum power.

12. What are turbochargers? (FAA-H-8083-25)

Higher performance aircraft typically operate at higher altitudes where air density is substantially less. The decrease in air density as altitude increases results in a decreased power output of an unsupercharged engine. By compressing the thin air by means of a supercharger, the turbocharged engine will maintain the preset power as altitude is increased. The turbocharger consists of a compressor to provide pressurized air to the engine, and a turbine driven by exhaust gases of the engine to drive the compressor.

13. What are cowl flaps? (AC 65-12A)

Cowl flaps are located on the engine cowling and allow the pilot to control the operating temperature of the engine by regulating the amount of air circulating within the engine compartment. Cowl flaps may be manually or electrically activated and usually allow for a variety of flap positions.

14. When are cowl flaps used? (AC 65-12A)

a. Normally the cowl flaps will be in the "open" position in the following operations:
- During starting of the engine
- While taxiing
- During takeoff and high-power climb operation

The cowl flaps may be adjusted in cruise flight for the appropriate cylinder head temperature.

b. The cowl flaps should be in the "closed" position in the following operations:
- During extended let-downs
- Anytime excessive cooling is a possibility (i.e., approach to landing, engine-out practice, etc.)

15. Define the term "service ceiling." (FAA-H-8083-25)

Service ceiling—Defined as the height above sea level beyond which the aircraft's maximum rate of climb would be no more than 100 feet per minute. The service ceiling may be found in the Pilot's Operating Handbook for that aircraft.

I. Propeller

1. What type of propeller does this aircraft have?

The airplane propeller may be described as

a. All-metal,

b. Two-bladed,

c. Constant-speed, and

d. Governor-regulated.

2. Discuss fixed-pitch propellers. (FAA-H-8083-25)

The pitch of this propeller is fixed by the manufacturer and cannot be changed by the pilot. Two types of fixed-pitch propellers are:

Climb propeller—has a lower pitch, therefore less drag. Results in higher rpm and more horsepower being developed by the engine; increases performance during takeoffs and climbs, but decreases performance during cruising flight.

Cruise propeller — has a higher pitch, therefore more drag. Results in lower rpm and less horsepower capability; decreases performance during takeoffs and climbs, but increases efficiency during cruising flight.

3. Discuss variable-pitch propellers (constant speed). (FAA-H-8083-25)

An airplane equipped with a constant-speed propeller is capable of continuously adjusting the propeller blade angle to maintain a constant engine speed. For example, if engine rpm increases as a result of a decreased load on the engine (descent), the system automatically increases the propeller blade angle (increasing air load) until the rpm has returned to the preset speed. The propeller governor can be regulated by the pilot with a control in the cockpit, so that any desired blade angle setting (within its limits) and engine operating rpm can be obtained, thereby increasing the airplane's efficiency in various flight conditions.

4. What does the propeller control do? (FAA-H-8083-25)

The propeller control regulates propeller pitch and engine rpm as desired for a given flight condition. The propeller control adjusts a propeller governor which establishes and maintains the propeller speed, which in turn maintains the engine speed.

5. What would the desired propeller setting be for maximum performance situations such as takeoff? (FAA-H-8083-25)

A low pitch, high rpm setting produces maximum power and thrust. The low blade angle keeps the angle of attack small and efficient with respect to the relative wind. At the same time, it allows the propeller to handle a smaller mass of air per revolution. This light load allows the engine to turn at high rpm and to convert the maximum amount of fuel into heat energy in a given time. The high rpm also creates maximum thrust because the mass of air handled per revolution is small, the number of revolutions per minute is many, the slipstream velocity is high, and the airplane speed is low.

6. What is a propeller governor? (AC 65-12A)

The propeller governor, with the assistance of a governor pump, controls the flow of engine oil to or from a piston in the propeller hub. When the engine oil, under high pressure from the governor pump, pushes the piston forward, the propeller blades are twisted toward a high pitch/low rpm condition. When the engine oil is released from the cylinder, centrifugal force, with the assistance of an internal spring, twists the blades towards a low pitch/high rpm condition.

7. **When operating an airplane with a constant-speed propeller, which condition induces the most stress on the engine?** (FAA-H-8083-3)

Excessive manifold pressure raises the cylinder compression pressure, resulting in high stresses within the engine. Excessive pressure also produces high engine temperatures. A combination of high manifold pressure and low rpm can induce damaging detonation; however, it is a fallacy that (in non-turbocharged engines) the manifold pressure in inches of mercury (inches Hg) should *never* exceed rpm in hundreds for cruise power settings. The cruise power charts in the AFM/POH should be consulted when selecting cruise power settings. Whatever the combinations of rpm and manifold pressure listed in these charts—they have been flight tested and approved by the airframe and powerplant engineers for the respective airframe and engine manufacturer.

J. Fuel System

1. **What type fuel system does this aircraft have?**

The fuel system consists of the following:

a. Two vented integral fuel tanks

b. A four-position fuel selector valve

c. A fuel strainer

d. A manual primer

e. An engine-driven fuel pump

f. An electric auxiliary fuel pump

g. A carburetor

The airplane uses a gravity-feed type fuel system. Fuel is delivered to the engine-driven fuel pump, unassisted, except by gravity. Fuel flows from the wing tanks to the fuel selector valve which is marked with BOTH, RIGHT, LEFT and OFF positions. From the fuel valve, fuel flows through a fuel strainer and then to the engine-driven fuel pump. The fuel pump then delivers fuel to the carburetor. After the carburetor, the fuel/air mixture is delivered to the cylinders via intake manifold tubes.

2. When is the auxiliary fuel boost pump used?

Proper usage of the fuel boost pump varies with different aircraft. In general, the fuel boost pump should be used during takeoffs and landings, when switching fuel tanks, and anytime fuel pressure falls below a selected value. The fuel boost pump in a Cessna 172-RG should be used anytime the fuel pressure falls below 0.5 PSI.

3. Why is it necessary to include a left and right position on the fuel selector valve?

During cruise flight, with the fuel selector valve on "Both," unequal fuel flow may occur if the wings are not consistently kept level during the flight. This will result in one wing being heavier than the other. A fuel selector valve with the left/right option allows a pilot to control the situation by selecting the tank on the heavier wing and remaining on that tank until both tanks contain approximately the same amount of fuel.

4. Where are the fuel vents located for each tank?

The left fuel tank is vented overboard through a vent line with a check valve. The right fuel tank is vented through the filler cap. Both fuel tanks are vented together by an interconnecting line.

5. What purpose do fuel tank vents have? (FAA-H-8083-25)

As the fuel level in an aircraft fuel tank decreases, without vents a vacuum would be created within the tank which would eventually result in a decreasing fuel flow and finally engine stoppage. Fuel system venting provides a way of replacing fuel with outside air, preventing formation of a vacuum.

6. What type fuel does this aircraft require (minimum octane rating and color)?

The approved fuel grade used is 100LL, and the color is blue.

7. Can other types of fuel be used if the specified grade is not available? (FAA-H-8083-25)

Airplane engines are designed to operate using a specific grade of fuel as recommended by the manufacturer. If the proper grade of fuel is not available, it is possible, but not desirable, to use the next higher grade as a substitute. If using a higher grade fuel than that specified as a minimum grade for your engine, the engine manufacturer's instructions must be observed. This is because the higher octane fuels normally used in higher-compression engines must ignite at higher temperatures—but not prematurely.

8. What are some examples of different fuel grades (octane ratings) available? (FAA-H-8083-25)

Grade	Color
80	Red
100	Green
100LL	Blue
Turbine	Colorless

Note: It is important to remember that if fuel grades are mixed together they will become clear or colorless.

9. What is the function of the manual primer, and how does it operate?

The manual primer's function is to provide assistance in starting the engine. The primer draws fuel from the fuel strainer and injects it directly into the cylinder intake ports. This usually results in a quicker, more efficient engine start.

10. Where are the drain valves located?

A drain valve is located on the bottom of each main wing and also directly under the fuel selector valve. A fuel strainer drain is located under an access panel on the right side of the engine cowling.

11. How is fuel quantity measured?

One float-type fuel quantity transmitter and one electric fuel quantity indicator measure fuel quantity for each tank.

12. Are the fuel quantity indicators accurate?
(FAA-H-8083-25)

Aircraft certification rules only require accuracy in fuel gauges when they read "empty." Any reading other than "empty" should be verified. Do not depend solely on the accuracy of the fuel quantity gauges. Always visually check the fuel level in each tank during the preflight inspection, and then compare it with the corresponding fuel quantity indication.

K. Oil System

1. Briefly describe the engine oil system.

Aircraft engine lubrication and oil for propeller governor operation is supplied from a sump on the bottom of the engine. Oil sump capacity is 8 quarts.

2. What are the minimum and maximum oil capacities?

The minimum oil capacity is 5 quarts of oil. The maximum oil capacity is 8 quarts.

3. What are the minimum and maximum oil temperatures and pressures?

Oil temperature—100°F to 245°F

Oil pressure—25 PSI (minimum for idling), 60 – 90 PSI (green arc), 115 PSI (red line)

4. What are two types of oil available for use in your airplane?

Mineral oil—Also known as non-detergent oil; contains no additives. This type of oil is normally used after an engine overhaul or when an aircraft engine is new; normally used for engine break-in purposes.

Ashless dispersant—Mineral oil with additives; high antiwear properties along with multi-viscosity (ability to perform in wide range of temps). Also picks up contamination and carbon particles and keeps them suspended so that buildups and sludge do not form in the engine.

5. **What type of oil is recommended for this engine (for summer and winter operations)?**

Ashless dispersant oil, usually SAE 20W-50 during the colder months. For temperatures above 60°F (summer), use SAE 40 or SAE 50.

L. Electrical System

1. Describe the electrical system on this aircraft.

Electrical energy is provided by a 28-volt, direct-current system, powered by an engine-driven 60-amp alternator and a 24-volt battery.

2. Where is the battery located?

The battery is located aft of the rear cabin wall.

3. How are the circuits for the various electrical accessories within the aircraft protected? (FAA-H-8083-25)

Most of the electrical circuits in an airplane are protected from an overload condition by either circuit breakers or fuses or both. Circuit breakers perform the same function as fuses except that when an overload occurs, a circuit breaker can be reset.

4. What is a bus bar? (FAA-H-8083-25)

A bus bar interfaces the electrical system with the various electrical accessories such as radios, lights, etc. A bus bar makes aircraft electrical wiring considerably less complex. Fuses or circuit breakers are incorporated into the bus bar providing protection for the different aircraft electrical circuits from possible damage as a result of faulty generators, alternators or components.

5. The electrical system provides power for what equipment in an airplane?

Normally the following:

a. Radio equipment

b. Turn coordinator

c. Fuel gauges

d. Pitot heat

e. Landing light

f. Taxi light

g. Strobe lights

h. Interior lights

i. Instrument lights

j. Position lights

k. Flaps (maybe)

l. Stall warning system (maybe)

m. Oil temperature gauge

n. Cigarette lighter (maybe)

6. What does the ammeter indicate? (FAA-H-8083-25)

It shows if the alternator/generator is producing an adequate supply of electrical power to the system by measuring the amperes of electricity, and also indicates whether the battery is receiving an electrical charge. If the needle indicates a plus value, it means that the battery is being charged. If the needle indicates a minus value, it means that the generator or alternator output is inadequate and energy is being drawn from the battery to supply the system.

7. What function does the voltage regulator have? (FAA-H-8083-25)

A voltage regulator controls the rate of charge to the battery by stabilizing the generator or alternator electrical output. The generator/alternator voltage output is usually slightly higher than the battery voltage. For example, a 12-volt battery would be fed by a generator/alternator system of approximately 14 volts. The difference in voltage keeps the battery charged.

8. Does the aircraft have an external power source receptacle, and if so where is it located?

Yes, the receptacle is located behind a door on the left side of the fuselage aft of the baggage compartment door.

9. What type of ignition system does your airplane have? (FAA-H-8083-25)

Engine ignition is provided by two engine-driven magnetos, and two spark plugs per cylinder. The ignition system is completely independent of the aircraft electrical system. The magnetos are self-contained units supplying electrical current without using an external source of power. However, before they can produce current, the magnetos must be actuated as the engine crankshaft is rotated by some other means. To accomplish this, the aircraft battery furnishes electrical power to operate a starter which, through a series of gears, rotates the engine crankshaft. This in turn actuates the armature of the magneto to produce the sparks for ignition of the fuel in each cylinder. After the engine starts, the starter system is disengaged and the battery no longer contributes to the actual operation of the engine.

10. What are the two main advantages of a dual ignition system? (FAA-H-8083-25)

a. Increased safety—in case one system fails the engine may be operated on the other until a landing is safely made.

b. More complete and even combustion of the mixture, and consequently improved engine performance; i.e., the fuel/air mixture will be ignited on each side of the combustion chamber and burn toward the center.

M. Environmental System

1. How does the aircraft cabin heat work?

Fresh air, heated by an exhaust shroud, is directed to the cabin
through a series of ducts.

2. How does the pilot control temperature in the cabin?

Temperature is controlled by mixing outside air (cabin air control)
with heated air (cabin heat control) in a manifold near the cabin
firewall. This air is then ducted to vents located on the cabin floor.

3. What are several types of oxygen systems in use? (FAA-H-8083-25)

Diluter-demand, pressure-demand, and continuous-flow.

4. Can any kind of oxygen be used for aviator's breathing oxygen? (FAA-H-8083-25)

No, oxygen used for medical purposes or welding normally should
not be used because it may contain too much water. The excess
water could condense and freeze in the oxygen lines when flying at
high altitudes. Specifications for "aviator's breathing oxygen" are
99.5% pure oxygen with not more than two milliliters of water per
liter of oxygen.

5. How does a continuous-flow oxygen system operate? (FAA-H-8083-25)

Continuous flow oxygen systems are usually provided for passengers. The passenger mask typically has a reservoir bag that collects
oxygen from the continuous flow oxygen system during the time
when the mask user is exhaling. The oxygen collected in the bag
allows a higher inspiratory flow rate during the inhalation cycle,
which reduces the amount of air dilution. Ambient air is added to
the supplied oxygen during inhalation after the reservoir bag oxygen supply is depleted. The exhaled air is released to the cabin.

6. How does a pressure demand oxygen system operate? (FAA-H-8083-25)

Pressure demand oxygen systems are similar to diluter demand oxygen equipment, except that oxygen is supplied to the mask under pressure at cabin altitudes above 34,000 feet. Pressure demand regulators create airtight and oxygen-tight seals, but they also provide a positive pressure application of oxygen to the mask face piece that allows the user's lungs to be pressurized with oxygen; this makes them safe at altitudes above 40,000 feet. Some systems may have a pressure demand mask with the regulator attached directly to the mask, rather than mounted on the instrument panel or other area within the flight deck.

7. What is a "pressurized" aircraft? (FAA-H-8083-25)

In a "pressurized" aircraft, the cabin, flight compartment, and baggage compartments are incorporated into a sealed unit which is capable of containing air under a pressure higher than outside atmospheric pressure. Pressurized air is pumped into this sealed fuselage by cabin superchargers which deliver a relatively constant volume of air at all altitudes up to a designed maximum. Air is released from the fuselage by a device called an outflow valve. Since the superchargers provide a constant inflow of air to the pressurized area, the outflow valve, by regulating the air exit, is the major controlling element in the pressurization system.

8. What operational advantages are there in flying pressurized aircraft? (FAA-H-8083-25)

A cabin pressurization system performs several functions:

a. It allows an aircraft to fly higher which can result in better fuel economy, higher speeds, and the capability to avoid bad weather and turbulence.

b. It will typically maintain a cabin pressure altitude of 8,000 feet at the maximum designed cruising altitude of the airplane.

c. It prevents rapid changes of cabin altitude which may be uncomfortable or injurious to passengers and crew.

d. It permits a reasonably fast exchange of air from inside to outside of the cabin. This is necessary to eliminate odors and to remove stale air.

9. Describe a typical cabin pressure control system. (FAA-H-8083-25)

The cabin pressure control system provides cabin pressure regulation, pressure relief, vacuum relief, and the means for selecting the desired cabin altitude in the isobaric and differential range. In addition, dumping of the cabin pressure is a function of the pressure control system. A cabin pressure regulator, an outflow valve, and a safety valve are used to accomplish these functions.

10. What are the components of a cabin pressure control system? (FAA-H-8083-25)

a. *Cabin pressure regulator*— Controls cabin pressure to a selected value in the isobaric range and limits cabin pressure to a preset differential value in the differential range.

b. *Cabin air pressure safety valve*—A combination pressure relief, vacuum relief, and dump valve.
   • Pressure relief valve: prevents cabin pressure from exceeding a predetermined differential pressure above ambient pressure.
   • Vacuum relief valve: prevents ambient pressure from exceeding cabin pressure by allowing external air to enter the cabin when the ambient pressure exceeds cabin pressure.
   • Dump valve: actuated by a cockpit control which will cause the cabin air to be dumped to the atmosphere.

c. *Instrumentation*—Several instruments used in conjunction with the pressurization controller are:
   • Cabin differential pressure gauge—Indicates difference between inside and outside pressure; should be monitored to ensure that the cabin does not exceed maximum allowable differential pressure.
   • Cabin altimeter—This is a check on system performance.

   Sometimes differential pressure and cabin altimeter combined into one:
   • Cabin rate-of-climb—Indicates cabin rate-of-climb or descent.

N. Deicing and Anti-Icing

1. What is the difference between a deice system and an anti-ice system? (AC 65-15A)

A deice system is used to eliminate ice that has already formed. An anti-ice system is used to prevent the formation of ice.

2. What types of systems are used in the prevention and elimination of airframe ice? (AC 65-15A)

Pneumatic—A deice type of system; consists of inflatable boots attached to the leading edges of the wings and tail surfaces. Compressed air from the pressure side of the engine vacuum pump is cycled through ducts or tubes in the boots causing the boots to inflate. Most systems also incorporate a timer.

Hot Air—An anti-ice type system; commonly found on turboprop and turbojet aircraft. Hot air is directed from the engine (compressor) to the leading edges of the wings.

3. What types of systems are used in the prevention and elimination of propeller ice? (AC 65-15A)

Electrically heated boots—Consist of heating elements incorporated into the boots which are bonded to the propeller. The ice buildup on the propeller is heated from below and then thrown off by centrifugal force.

Fluid system—Consists of an electrically driven pump which, when activated, supplies a fluid, such as alcohol, to a device in the propeller spinner which distributes the fluid along the propeller assisted by centrifugal force.

4. What types of systems are used in the prevention and elimination of windshield ice? (AC 65-15A)

Fluid system—Consists of an electrically-driven pump which may be activated to spray a fluid, such as alcohol, onto the windshield to prevent the formation of ice.

Electrical system—Heating elements are embedded in the windshield or in a device attached to the windshield which when activated, prevents the formation of ice.

O. Avionics

1. What function does the avionics power switch have?

The avionics power switch controls power from the primary bus to
the avionics bus. The circuit is protected by a combination power
switch/circuit breaker. Aircraft avionics are isolated from electrical
power when the switch is in the "Off" position. Also, if an overload should occur in the system, the avionics power switch will
move to the "Off" position, causing an interruption of power to all
aircraft avionics.

2. What are static dischargers? (AC 65-15A)

Static dischargers are installed on aircraft to reduce radio receiver
interference caused by corona discharge, which is emitted from the
aircraft as a result of precipitation static. Static dischargers, normally mounted on the trailing edges of the control surfaces, wing
tips, and vertical stabilizer, discharge the precipitation static at
points a critical length away from the wing and tail extremities
where there is little or no coupling of the static into the radio
antenna.

3. Within what frequency band does the following type of navigational and communication equipment installed on board most aircraft operate? (AIM)

VOR receiver (VHF band)..............................108.0 to 117.95 MHz

Communication transceivers (VHF band)......118.0 to 136.975
MHz

DME receiver (UHF band) ....960 MHz to 1215
MHz

ADF receiver (LF to MF band)......................190 to 530 kHz

Note: Know the location and function of the various antennas on
your aircraft!

Additional Study Questions

1. During a preflight runup, the pilot switches from both magnetos to the left magneto and notes there is no drop in rpm. What does this indicate? (FAA-H-8083-25)

2. A pilot notices that when applying carburetor heat during an engine runup on the ground, an increase in rpm occurs. What does this indicate? (FAA-H-8083-25)

3. What is the purpose of "differential" aileron travel? (AC 65-15A)

4. The attitude and heading indicator contains several markings. What information do they provide? (FAA-H-8083-25)

5. During gear extension or retraction, the electric hydraulic pump malfunctions and continues to run after the gear has been extended or retracted. How would the pilot detect this malfunction? (POH)

6. Where is the hydraulic reservoir located on your aircraft? What type fluid does it use? (POH)

7. What indications will you have if a loss of hydraulic pressure occurs in flight? (POH)

8. What is the maximum number of degrees the nose wheel will travel left or right of center? (POH)

9. Where are the brake system master cylinder(s) located on your aircraft? (POH)

10. If a loss of oil pressure in the propeller occurs, what effect will this have on the propeller pitch and rpm? (POH)

Emergency
Procedures

4

Some of the following questions are in reference to the systems of a Cessna 172-RG. For accuracy, a review of your aircraft's Pilot Operating Handbook should be made.

A. Spin Recovery

1. What is the recommended procedure for recovery from a spin? (FAA-H-8083-3)

In the absence of the manufacturer's recommended spin recovery procedures and techniques, the following spin recovery procedures are recommended.

a. Reduce the power (throttle) to idle.

b. Position the ailerons to neutral.

c. Apply full opposite rudder against the rotation.

d. Apply a positive and brisk, straightforward movement of the elevator control forward of the neutral position to break the stall.

e. After spin rotation stops, neutralize the rudder.

f. Begin applying back-elevator pressure to raise the nose to level flight.

2. What does an aft center of gravity do to an aircraft's spin characteristics? (FAA-H-8083-25)

Recovery from a stall in any aircraft becomes progressively more difficult as its center of gravity moves aft. This is particularly important in spin recovery, as there is a point in rearward loading of any airplane at which a "flat" spin will develop. A "flat" spin is one in which centrifugal force acting through a center of gravity located well to the rear, will pull the tail of the airplane out away from the axis of the spin, making it impossible to get the nose down and recover.

3. **What load factor is present in a spin?** (AC 61-67)

The load factor during a spin will vary with the spin characteristics of each airplane but is usually found to be slightly above the 1G load of level flight. There are two reasons this is true:

a. The airspeed in a spin is very low (usually within 2 knots of the unaccelerated stalling speed); and

b. The airplane pivots, rather than turns, while it is in a spin.

B. Emergency Checklist

Discuss the use of an emergency checklist.

In the event of an in-flight emergency, the pilot should be sufficiently familiar with emergency procedures to take immediate action instinctively to prevent more serious situations from occurring. However, as soon as circumstances permit, the emergency checklist should be reviewed to ensure that all required items have been checked. Additionally, before takeoff, a pilot should be sure that the emergency checklist will be readily accessible in flight if needed.

C. Partial Power Loss

What procedures should be followed concerning a partial loss of power in flight? (POH)

If a partial loss of power occurs, the first priority is to establish and maintain a suitable airspeed (best glide airspeed if necessary).

Then, select an emergency landing area and remain within gliding distance. As time allows, attempt to determine the cause and correct it. Complete the following checklist:

a. Check the carburetor heat.

b. Check the amount of fuel in each tank and switch fuel tanks if necessary.

c. Check the fuel selector valve's current position.

d. Check the mixture control.

e. Check that the primer control is all the way in and locked.

f. Check the operation of the magnetos in all three positions: both, left or right.

D. Engine Failure

1. In the event of a complete engine failure on takeoff, what procedure is recommended? (POH)

If an engine failure occurs during the takeoff run, the following checklist should be completed:

a. Retard the throttle to idle.

b. Apply pressure to the brakes.

c. Retract the wing flaps.

d. Set the mixture control to "Idle Cut-off."

e. Turn the ignition switch to "Off."

f. Turn the master switch to "Off."

2. If an engine failure occurs immediately after takeoff, what procedure is recommended? (POH)

If an engine failure occurs immediately after takeoff, and before a safe maneuvering altitude is attained, it is usually inadvisable to attempt to turn back to the field from which the takeoff was made. Instead, it is generally safer to immediately establish the proper glide attitude, and select a field directly ahead or slightly to either side of the takeoff path.

The following checklist should be completed:

a. Establish an airspeed of 70 KIAS (flaps up) or 65 KIAS (flaps down).

b. Set mixture to "Idle Cut-off."

c. Set fuel selector valve to "Off."

d. Set ignition switch to "Off."

e. Set wing flaps as required (30 degrees is recommended).

f. Set master switch "Off."

3. **What is the recommended procedure to be followed for an engine failure while en route?** (POH)

   The first priority is to establish a best-glide airspeed. Then, select an emergency landing area and remain within gliding distance. As time permits, try to determine the cause of the failure (no fuel, carburetor ice, etc.). Attempt an engine restart if possible. The recommended checklist for this procedure is:

   a. Establish an airspeed of 75 KIAS.

   b. Set carburetor heat on.

   c. Set the fuel selector valve to "Both."

   d. Set the mixture control to "Rich."

   e. Turn the ignition switch to "Both"; if the propeller has stopped, turn the ignition switch to "Start."

   f. Check that the primer control is pushed in and is "Locked."

4. **What is the recommended power-off gliding speed in an engine-out procedure?** (POH)

   73 KIAS at 2,650 pounds.

E. Emergency Landing

1. **If an engine failure has occurred while en route and a forced landing is imminent, what procedures should be followed?** (POH)

   a. Establish an airspeed of 75 KIAS.

   b. Begin a scan for an appropriate field for landing using the following order of preference:
      • Paved airport
      • Unpaved airport
      • Paved road with no obstacles
      • Unpaved road with no obstacles
      • Grass field
      • Plowed field
      • Lakes or ponds
      • Trees or other structures

c. Attempt an engine restart.

d. Set your transponder to "7700."

e. Transmit a "mayday" message on either the frequency in use or 121.5.

f. Begin to spiral down over the approach end of the selected landing site.

g. On your final approach complete the forced landing checklist.

2. Immediately before touchdown in a forced landing procedure, what items should be completed?

The Emergency Landing Checklist should be completed:

a. Establish an airspeed with flaps up of 75 KIAS and with flaps down of 65 KIAS.

b. Set the mixture control to "Idle Cut-Off."

c. Set the fuel selector valve to "Off."

d. Turn the ignition switch to "Off."

e. Select the landing down or up depending on terrain.

f. Set the wing flaps as required (30 degrees is recommended).

g. Make sure doors are unlatched prior to touchdown.

h. Turn the master switch to "Off."

i. Make your touchdown with the tail slightly low.

j. Apply brakes heavily.

3. In an engine failure situation, what glide ratio will be obtained if the best-glide airspeed is maintained?

A loss of 600 feet per 1 nautical mile (i.e., an aircraft at 3,000 feet AGL would have a maximum gliding distance of 5 miles).

4. If a forced landing is imminent, should the landing gear be left up, or down and locked? (FAA-H-8083-3)

There can't be a hard and fast rule concerning the position of a retractable landing gear at touchdown. In rugged terrain and trees, or during impacts at high sink rate, an extended gear would definitely have a protective effect on the cockpit/cabin area. But weigh this advantage against the possible side effects of a collapsing gear, such as a ruptured fuel tank. As always, the manufacturer's recommendations as outlined in the AFM/POH should be followed. When a normal touchdown is assured, and ample stopping distance is available, a gear-up landing on level-but-soft terrain, or across a plowed field, may result in less airplane damage than a gear-down landing.

5. If an engine failure has occurred while over water, and you are beyond power-off gliding distance to land, what procedures should be followed? (POH)

a. Set your transponder to "7700" and broadcast a "mayday" message on the frequency in use or 121.5 MHz.

b. Make sure all heavy objects are secured or, if possible, jettison them.

c. Select landing gear up.

d. Set flaps to 20–30 degrees.

e. Set power (if available) so as to establish 300 fpm descent and 60 KIAS.

f. Approach and land parallel to heavy sea swells when in light winds, and approach and land into the wind when high winds and heavy seas exist.

g. If no power is available establish an approach airspeed of 70 KIAS with flaps up or 65 KIAS with 10 degrees flap.

h. Open all cabin doors prior to touchdown.

i. Initiate your touchdown in a level flight attitude.

j. Just prior to touchdown, protect body with life vests, clothing, etc.

k. After touchdown, begin evacuation of the airplane. Open the windows to equalize pressure if the doors do not open easily.

l. Inflate life vests and raft if available.

F. Engine Roughness or Overheat

1. What is detonation? (FAA-H-8083-15)

Detonation is an uncontrolled, explosive ignition of the fuel/air mixture within the cylinder's combustion chamber. It causes excessive temperatures and pressures which, if not corrected, can quickly lead to failure of the piston, cylinder, or valves. In less severe cases, detonation causes engine overheating, roughness, or loss of power. It is characterized by high cylinder head temperatures, and is most likely to occur when operating at high power settings.

2. What are some of the most common operational causes of detonation? (FAA-H-8083-25)

a. Using a lower fuel grade than that specified by the aircraft manufacturer.

b. Operating with extremely high manifold pressures in conjunction with low rpm.

c. Operating the engine at high power settings with an excessively lean mixture.

d. Extended ground operations or steep climbs where cylinder cooling is reduced.

3. What action should be taken if detonation is suspected? (FAA-H-8083-25)

Detonation may be avoided by following these basic guidelines during the various phases of ground and flight operations:

a. Make sure the proper grade of fuel is being used.

b. While on the ground, keep the cowl flaps (if available) in the full-open position.

c. During takeoff and initial climb, use an enriched fuel mixture, as well as a shallower climb angle to increase cylinder cooling.

d. Avoid extended, high power, steep climbs.

e. Develop habit of monitoring engine instruments to verify proper operation.

4. What is preignition? (FAA-H-8083-25)

Preignition occurs when the fuel/air mixture ignites prior to the engine's normal ignition event. Premature burning is usually caused by a residual hot spot in the combustion chamber, often created by a small carbon deposit on a spark plug, a cracked spark plug insulator, or other damage in the cylinder that causes a part to heat sufficiently to ignite the fuel/air charge. Preignition causes the engine to lose power, and produces high operating temperature. As with detonation, preignition may also cause severe engine damage, because the expanding gases exert excessive pressure on the piston while still on its compression stroke.

5. What actions should be taken if preignition is suspected? (FAA-H-8083-25)

Detonation and preignition often occur simultaneously and one may cause the other. Since either condition causes high engine temperature accompanied by a decrease in engine performance, it is often difficult to distinguish between the two. Using the recommended grade of fuel, and operating the engine within its proper temperature, pressure, and rpm ranges, reduces the chance of detonation or preignition.

6. If the engine begins to run rough when flying through heavy rain, what action should be taken?

During flight through heavy rain, it is possible for the induction air filter to become water saturated. This situation will reduce the amount of available air to the carburetor resulting in an excessively rich mixture and a corresponding loss of power. Carburetor heat may be used as an alternate source of air in such a situation.

7. Are there any special considerations necessary when using the auxiliary pump after an engine-driven fuel pump failure? (POH)

In a high-wing, single-engine aircraft, which has sustained an engine-driven fuel pump failure, gravity flow will provide sufficient fuel flow for level or descending flight. If the failure occurs while in a climb or the fuel pressure falls below 0.5 PSI, the auxiliary fuel pump should be used.

8. What operating procedure could be used to minimize spark plug fouling?

Engine roughness may occur due to "fouling" of the spark plug electrodes. This condition may occur on the ground or in the air and is usually the result of an excessively rich mixture setting which causes unburned carbon and lead deposits to collect on the spark plug electrodes. A pilot may alleviate this problem to some degree by always using the recommended lean setting for the given condition.

G. Loss of Oil Pressure

1. During a cross-country flight you notice that the oil pressure is low, but the oil temperature is normal. What is the problem and what action should be taken?

A low oil pressure in flight could be the result of any one of several problems, the most common being that of insufficient oil. If the oil temperature continues to remain normal, a clogged oil pressure relief valve or an oil pressure gauge malfunction could be the culprit. In any case, a landing at the nearest airport is advisable to check for the cause of the trouble.

2. If a loss of oil pressure occurs accompanied by a rising oil temperature, what is indicated? (FAA-H-8083-25)

The oil required for cooling has been lost, and an engine failure is imminent. The throttle should be reduced, and a suitable landing area should be established as soon as possible. Use minimum power to reach the emergency landing area.

H. Smoke and Fire

1. What procedure should be followed if an engine fire develops on the ground during starting? (POH)

Continue to attempt an engine start as a start will cause flames and excess fuel to be sucked back through the carburetor.

a. *If the engine starts:*
   - Increase the power to a higher rpm for a few moments; and then
   - Shut down the engine and inspect it.

b. *If the engine does not start:*
   - Set the throttle to the "Full" position.
   - Set the mixture control to "Idle cutoff."
   - Continue to try an engine start in an attempt to put out the fire by vacuum.

c. *If the fire continues:*
   - Obtain fire extinguisher and/or fire personnel assistance
   - Turn the master switch to "Off."
   - Turn the ignition switch to "Off."
   - Set the fuel selector to "Off."
   - Extinguish the fire using extinguisher

Evacuate the aircraft and obtain a fire extinguisher and/or fire personnel assistance.

2. What procedure should be followed if an engine fire develops in flight? (POH)

In the event of an engine fire in flight, the following procedure should be used:

a. Set the mixture control to "Idle cutoff."

b. Set the fuel selector valve to "Off."

c. Turn the master switch to "Off."

d. Set the cabin heat and air vents to "Off;" leave the overhead vents "On."

e. Establish an airspeed of 105 KIAS and increase the descent, if necessary, to find an airspeed that will provide for an incombustible mixture.

f. Execute a forced landing procedures checklist.

3. What procedure should be followed if an electrical fire develops inside the aircraft? (POH)

If an electrical fire is suspected (burning odor), the pilot should initially try to identify the possible source by checking all circuit breakers, avionics and instruments. If the problem is not detected and the odor or smoke continues, the following checklist should be completed:

a. Turn the master switch to "Off."

b. Set the avionics power switch to "Off."

c. Set all other switches to "Off" except the ignition switch.

d. Close all air/heat vents as well as any other air vents.

e. Use fire extinguisher.

4. What troubleshooting procedure should be followed in determining the cause of an electrical fire that is not readily apparent? (POH)

a. Turn the master switch "On."

b. Check all the circuit breakers for their status.

c. Check all radio switches are "Off."

d. Turn avionics power switch "On."

e. Turn radio and electrical switches "On" one at a time with delay after each to isolate which circuit is tripping the breaker and/or causing the burning odor.

f. Open all air vents once fire is extinguished.

5. What procedure should be followed if a cabin fire develops in flight? (POH)

Typically cabin fires are electrical in nature and identifying and disabling the faulty circuit is the first priority. However, careless smoking by passengers has also been a significant cause of cabin fires. The following checklist should be completed:

a. Turn the master switch to "Off."

b. Close all air/heat vents.

c. Use a fire extinguisher if available.

d. Land as soon as possible.

6. What procedure should be followed if a wing fire develops in flight? (POH)

If a wing fire develops in flight, the following checklist should be completed:

a. Set the navigation light switch to "Off."

b. Set the strobe light switch to "Off."

c. Set the pitot heat switch to "Off."

Initiate a sideslip maneuver to avoid flames from getting to the fuel tank and cabin area, then land as soon as possible.

I. Icing

1. What are the three main types of aircraft icing? (AC 00-6A)

Structural, induction system, and instrument icing.

2. Name four types of structural ice. (AC 00-6A)

Clear ice — Forms when large drops strike the aircraft surface and slowly freeze.

Rime ice — Small drops strike the aircraft and freeze rapidly.

Mixed ice — A combination of the above; usually supercooled water drops varying in size.

Frost — Ice crystal deposits formed by sublimation when the temperature at the surface is below the dew point, and the dew point is below freezing.

3. What is necessary for structural icing to occur? (AC 00-6A)

The aircraft must be flying through visible water such as rain or cloud droplets; temperature must be at the point where moisture strikes the aircraft at 0°C or colder.

4. Which type of structural icing is more dangerous, rime or clear? (AC 00-6A)

Clear ice is hard, heavy, and tenacious. It is typically the most hazardous ice encountered. Clear ice forms when, after initial impact, the remaining liquid portion of the drop flows out over the aircraft surface, gradually freezing as a smooth sheet of solid ice. This type forms when drops are large, as in rain or in cumuliform clouds. Its removal by deicing equipment is especially difficult due to the fact that it forms as it flows away from the deicing equipment (inflatable boots, etc.).

5. What action is recommended if you inadvertently encounter icing conditions? (AC 00-6A)

You should change course and/or altitude; usually, climb to a higher altitude.

6. If icing has been inadvertently encountered, how would your landing approach procedure be different?

The following guidelines may be used when flying an airplane which has accumulated ice:

a. Maintain more power during the approach than normal.

b. Maintain a higher airspeed than normal.

c. Expect a higher stall speed than normal.

d. Expect a longer landing roll than normal.

e. A "no flaps" approach is recommended.

f. Maintain a consistently higher altitude than normal.

g. Avoid a missed approach (get it right the first time).

7. Which type of precipitation will produce the most hazardous icing conditions?

Freezing rain produces the most hazardous icing conditions.

8. Does the stall warning system have any protection from ice? (POH)

No, but some aircraft may be equipped with a heated stall warning system which consists of a vane, sensor unit and heating element on the leading edge of the wing. Usually this system is activated by the same switch that controls the pitot heat.

9. What causes carburetor icing and what are the first indications of its presence? (FAA-H-8083-25)

The vaporization of fuel, combined with the expansion of air as it passes through the carburetor, causes a sudden cooling of the mixture. The temperature of the air passing through the carburetor may drop as much as 60°F within a fraction of a second. Water vapor is squeezed out by this cooling, and, if the temperature in the carburetor reaches 32°F or below, the moisture will be deposited as frost or ice inside the carburetor.

For airplanes with a fixed pitch propeller, the first indication of carburetor icing is a loss of rpm. For airplanes with controllable-pitch (constant speed) propellers, the first indication is usually a drop in manifold pressure.

10. What conditions are favorable for carburetor icing?
(FAA-H-8083-25)

Carburetor ice is most likely to occur when temperatures are below 70°F (21°C) and the relative humidity is above 80 percent. However, due to the sudden cooling that takes place in the carburetor, icing can occur even with temperatures as high as 100°F (38°C) and humidity as low as 50 percent. This temperature drop can be as much as 60 to 70°F. Therefore, at an outside air temperature of 100°F, a temperature drop of 70°F results in an air temperature in the carburetor of 30°F.

J. Pressurization

1. What is meant by decompression? (FAA-H-8083-25)

Decompression is the inability of the aircraft's pressurization system to maintain the designed "aircraft cabin" pressure. For example, an aircraft is flying at an altitude of 29,000 feet but the aircraft cabin is pressurized to an altitude equivalent to 8,000 feet. If decompression occurs, the cabin pressure may become equivalent to that of the aircraft's altitude of 29,000 feet. The rate at which this occurs determines the severity of decompression.

2. What are the two types of decompression?
(FAA-H-8083-25)

Explosive decompression—Cabin pressure decreases faster than the lungs can decompress. Most authorities consider any kind of decompression which occurs in less than $\frac{1}{2}$ second as explosive and potentially dangerous. This type of decompression could only be caused by structural damage, material failure, or by a door "popping" open.

Rapid decompression—A change in cabin pressure where the lungs decompress faster than the cabin. There is no likelihood of lung damage in this case. This type could be caused by a failure or malfunction in the pressurization system itself, or through slow leaks in the pressurized area.

3. What are the dangers of decompression? (FAA-H-8083-25)

a. Hypoxia

b. At higher altitudes, being tossed or blown out of the airplane

c. Evolved gas decompression sickness (the bends)

d. Exposure to wind blast and extreme cold

K. Emergency Descent

1. When would an emergency descent procedure be necessary? (FAA-H-8083-3)

An emergency descent is a maneuver for descending as rapidly as possible, within the structural limitations of the airplane, to a lower altitude or to the ground for an emergency landing. The need for this maneuver may result from an uncontrollable fire, a sudden loss of cabin pressurization, or any other situation demanding an immediate and rapid descent.

2. What procedure should be followed in establishing an emergency descent? (FAA-H-8083-3)

Generally the maneuver should be configured as recommended by the manufacturer. Except when prohibited by the manufacturer, the following procedure may be used:

a. Reduce power to idle;

b. Place propeller control in low pitch (high rpm)—acts as an aerodynamic brake;

c. As quickly as practical, extend landing gear/full flaps (maximum drag);

d. Establish a 30- to 45-degree bank for the purposes of clearing the area below.

L. Pitot/Static System and Associated Flight Instruments

1. What instruments are affected when the pitot tube freezes? (FAA-H-8083-25)

a. *Pitot tube blocked and associated drain hole remains clear* — Airspeed decreases to zero, altimeter and vertical speed read normal.

b. *Pitot tube and drain hole blocked* — Airspeed indicator acts as an altimeter; reads high in climb and low in descent. Altimeter and vertical speed read normal.

2. What instruments are affected when the static port freezes? (FAA-H-8083-25)

Airspeed Indicator — Accurate at the altitude frozen as long as the static pressure in the indicator and the system equals outside pressure. If the aircraft descends, the airspeed indicator would read high (outside static pressure greater than that trapped). If the aircraft climbs, the airspeed indicator will read low.

Altimeter — Indicates the altitude at which the system was blocked.

Vertical speed — Indicates level flight.

3. Does the pitot system have any protection from ice?

Yes. The heated pitot system consists of the following components:

a. A pitot tube with a heating element,

b. A "pitot heat" rocker switch, and

c. A 10-amp push-to-reset circuit breaker.

4. What corrective action is needed if the pitot tube freezes? If the static port freezes? (FAA-H-8083-25)

Pitot tube — Turn pitot heat on.

Static port — Use alternate air if available, or break the face of a static instrument (either the VSI or A/S indicator).

5. What indications should you expect while using alternate air? (FAA-H-8083-25)

In many unpressurized aircraft equipped with a pitot-static tube, an alternate source of static pressure is provided for emergency use. If the alternate source is vented inside the airplane, where static pressure is usually lower than outside, selection of the alternate static source may result in the following indications:

Altimeter .... will indicate higher than the actual altitude

Airspeed .... will indicate greater than the actual airspeed

Vertical speed .... will indicate a climb while in level flight

Note: Always consult the AFM/POH to determine the amount of error.

M. Vacuum System and Associated Flight Instruments

1. What instruments may be relied upon in the event of a complete vacuum system failure while operating in instrument meteorological conditions?

Turn and Slip/Turn Coordinator—bank information

Magnetic Compass—bank information

Airspeed—pitch information

Altimeter—pitch information

Vertical Speed Indicator—pitch information

2. Is there a backup system available if the engine-driven vacuum pump were to fail?

Some general aviation aircraft may be equipped with a backup vacuum system. This system may be electrically driven or could be an engine-driven vacuum pump running in parallel to the primary pump.

N. Electrical

1. What recommended procedure should be used in resetting a tripped circuit breaker? (POH)

Circuit breakers may be reset, but allow for a short cooling period to occur first (2 minutes). If, after resetting the circuit breaker, it pops out again, the circuit should be disabled and the circuit breaker left out.

2. Interpret the following ammeter indications. (POH)

a. Ammeter indicates a right deflection (positive).
After starting—The power from the battery used for starting is being replenished by the alternator. Or, if a full-scale charge is indicated for more than 1 minute, the starter is still engaged and a shutdown is indicated.

During flight—A faulty voltage regulator is causing the alternator to overcharge the battery.

b. Ammeter indicates a left deflection (negative).
After starting—Normal during start. Other times indicates the alternator is not functioning or an overload condition has occurred in the system. The battery is not receiving a charge.

During flight—The alternator is not functioning or an overload has occurred in the system. The battery is not receiving a charge.

3. What action should be taken if the ammeter indicates a continuous discharge (left needle) while in flight?

The alternator has quit producing a charge, so the master switch and the alternator circuit breaker should be checked and reset if necessary. If this does not correct the problem, the following should be accomplished:

a. The alternator should be turned off; pull the circuit breaker (field circuit will continue to draw power from the battery).

b. All electrical equipment not essential to flight should be turned off (the battery is now the only source of electrical power).

c. The flight should be terminated and a landing made as soon as possible.

4. What action should be taken if the ammeter indicates a continuous charge (right needle) while in flight (more than two needle widths)? (POH)

If a continuous excessive rate of charge were allowed for any extended period of time, the battery would overheat and evaporate the electrolyte at an excessive rate. A possible explosion of the battery could result. Also, electronic components in the electrical system would be adversely affected by higher than normal voltage. Protection is provided by an overvoltage sensor which will shut the alternator down if an excessive voltage is detected. If this should occur the following should be done:

a. The alternator should be turned off; pull the circuit breaker (the field circuit will continue to draw power from the battery).

b. All electrical equipment not essential to flight should be turned off (the battery is now the only source of electrical power).

c. The flight should be terminated and a landing made as soon as possible.

5. If the low-voltage warning light illuminates, what has occurred? (POH)

Illumination of the low-voltage light along with a discharge indication on the ammeter can occur during low rpm conditions with a full electrical load on the system. This event usually occurs on the ground with low rpms while taxiing. Another possibility is the alternator has been shutdown; the airplane is equipped with a combination alternator/regulator high-low voltage control unit which, when an over-voltage condition occurs, will shut down the alternator and illuminate the warning light. The battery is now supplying all current to the electrical system. The ammeter will indicate a discharge.

O. Landing Gear

1. If a positive gear down indication is not received, what action is recommended first? (POH)

Several preliminary checks can be made prior to using the emergency extension procedure:

a. Check that the master switch is set to "On."

b. Check that the "Landing Gear" and "Gear Pump" circuit breakers are in.

c. Check both "Landing Gear" position indicators by using the "Press-To-Test" feature and by rotating the dimming shutter.

d. If a bulb has burned out, you can use the other operating bulb as a temporary replacement.

2. What recommended procedure should be used if the landing gear fails to retract after takeoff? (POH)

If the landing gear fails to retract normally, the following checklist should be completed.

a. Check that the master switch is set to "On."

b. Check that the landing gear lever is in the full up position.

c. Check that the gear pump and landing gear circuit breakers are "In."

d. Check the gear up light.

e. Recycle the landing gear lever.

f. Check for proper gear motor operation by examining the ammeter and listening for noise.

Note: If you still hear a gear motor noise after 1 minute, pull out the gear pump circuit breaker to avoid overheating the motor. You can reinstall the circuit breaker when needed for landing.

3. How is the emergency gear extension system operated?

There is a hand-operated pump, located between the front seats, which may be used for manual extension of the landing gear in the event of a hydraulic failure.

4. What is the recommended procedure if the landing gear will not extend normally? (POH)

If the landing gear fails to extend normally, the following checklist should be completed.

a. Check that the master switch is "On."

b. Check that the landing gear lever is "Down."

c. Check that the gear pump and landing gear circuit breakers are "In."

d. Extend the handle and pump the emergency hand pump until heavy resistance is encountered (about 30–40 times).

e. Check that the gear down light is "On."

f. Secure the pump handle.

5. What procedure should be followed if a pilot does not receive a positive indication of the gear being down and locked? (POH)

Attempt to extend the gear manually. If this action is unsuccessful, plan for a gear-up landing. The following checklist should be completed:

a. Complete the "before landing" checklist.

b. Establish a normal approach configuration with full flaps.

c. Check that the gear pump and landing gear circuit breakers are "In."

d. Initiate a tail low landing.

e. Use a minimum amount of braking.

f. Taxi slowly.

g. Shut down the engine and then inspect the gear.

6. What is the recommended procedure in dealing with a flat main landing gear tire? (POH)

a. Establish a normal approach configuration with full flaps.

b. Touchdown with the good tire first on that side of the runway and keep the aircraft off of the flat tire for as long as possible.

c. Use braking on the good wheel as required to maintain directional control.

7. What is the recommended procedure to follow if the nose gear is unsafe or the tire is flat? (POH)

a. Complete the before landing checklist.

b. Shift weight to the rear by moving passengers and/or baggage to the rear.

c. Set the flaps to the 30° position.

d. Unlatch all doors.

e. After committing to a landing, set both the avionics and master switch to the "Off" position.

f. Initiate touchdown in a slightly tail low configuration.

g. Set the mixture control to the "Idle-Cutoff" position.

h. Set the ignition switch to the "Off" position.

i. Set the fuel selector to the "Off" position.

j. Hold the nose off as long as possible.

k. After landing, evacuate the aircraft as soon as possible.

8. Why should taxiing on a slush, snow, or ice covered taxiway in a retractable gear airplane be avoided? (AC 91-13)

During thawing conditions, mud and slush can be thrown into wheel wells during taxiing and takeoff. If it then freezes during flight, this mud and slush could create landing gear operational problems. The practice of recycling the gear after a takeoff can be used as a preventive procedure. However, the safest procedure is to avoid these surface conditions with retractable gear aircraft.

P. Wing Flaps (Asymmetrical Position)

1. What is an "asymmetrical" flap emergency? (FAA-H-8083-3)

An asymmetric "split" flap situation is one in which one flap deploys or retracts while the other remains in position. The problem is indicated by a pronounced roll toward the wing with the least flap deflection when wing flaps are extended or retracted.

2. What procedure should be followed in an asymmetrical flap emergency? (FAA-H-8083-3)

The roll encountered in a split flap situation is countered with opposite aileron. The yaw caused by the additional drag created by the extended flap will require substantial opposite rudder, resulting in a cross-control condition. Almost full aileron may be required to maintain a wings-level attitude, especially at the reduced airspeed necessary for approach and landing. The approach to landing with a split flap condition should be flown at a higher than normal airspeed. The pilot should not risk an asymmetric stall and subsequent loss of control by flaring excessively. The airplane should be flown onto the runway so that the touchdown occurs at an airspeed consistent with a safe margin above flaps-up stall speed.

Q. Inoperative Elevator

What procedure should be followed if loss of elevator control occurs? (POH)

a. Extend the landing gear.

b. Lower flaps by 10°.

c. Set trim for level flight.

d. Using throttle and elevator trim control, establish an airspeed of 70 knots.

Do not change the established trim setting. Maintain control of the glide angle by adjusting power. At the landing flare, the elevator trim should be adjusted to full noseup and the power reduced. At the moment of touchdown, close the throttle.

R. Inadvertent Door Opening

1. What procedure should be followed if a cabin door accidentally opens in flight? (POH)

a. Establish a straight-and-level flight configuration.

b. Trim the aircraft for approximately 80 KIAS.

c. Open a window.

d. Momentarily push the door outward and then pull the door to closed position and lock.

2. What procedure should be followed if a baggage door opens in flight? (POH)

Baggage compartments tend to be located in the aft section of the airplane and under no circumstances should the pilot allow anyone to attempt to close the doors while in flight. By design, the baggage compartment door will tend to remain closed during flight due to airflow pressure.

S. Emergency Equipment and Survival Gear

1. What two factors should be considered in choosing the type of survival equipment to carry for a flight over an uninhabited area? (AIM 6-2-7)

a. The type of climate

b. The type of terrain

2. What additional equipment is required if an aircraft is operated for hire over water and beyond power-off gliding distance from shore? (14 CFR 91.205)

If an aircraft is operated for hire over water and beyond power-off gliding distance from shore, approved flotation gear readily available to each occupant and at least one pyrotechnic signaling device.

3. **What do you have in the aircraft that can be used to aid in survival?**

   a. The compass will keep you going in one direction.

   b. Gasoline will help make a fire.

   c. Oil can be used for smoke signals.

   d. Seat upholstery may be used to wrap around feet or hands.

   e. Wiring may be used for tie strings.

   f. The battery may be used to ignite fuel.

Additional Study Questions

1. **In the event of an emergency requiring a forced landing, what information should be included in the "emergency" briefing to the passengers?** (POH)

2. **If an engine failure occurs immediately after takeoff, why is it inadvisable to turn back to the departure runway for landing?** (FAA-H-8083-3)

3. **During an emergency landing you realize that you have misjudged the glidepath and will "overshoot" the forced landing area. What procedures should be used? What procedures should be used for an "undershoot"?** (FAA-H-8083-3)

4. **What effect does the wind have on an emergency approach and landing procedure?** (FAA-H-8083-3)

5. **If the landing gear will not retract normally, can you retract the gear manually? How?** (POH)

6. **You have just extended the landing gear manually due to a hydraulic system failure (suspected loss of hydraulic fluid). Should you expect to also have braking problems on the landing rollout?** (POH)

7. If the alternator has failed and the battery is the only source of electrical power, approximately how much time remains before a complete electrical system failure occurs? What factors will affect the time remaining? (POH)

8. What flight instrument indications would you see if both the pitot static tube and static port became blocked for some reason? (FAA-H-8083-15)

9. What procedures should you use if the trim control on your aircraft has become inoperative, resulting in excessive control pressures inflight? (POH)

10. Are fuel injected engines subject to induction system icing? (FAA-H-8083-25)

Performance
and Limitations

5

A. Structure of the Atmosphere

1. How is aircraft performance significantly affected as air becomes less dense? (FAA-H-8083-25)

As air becomes less dense, it reduces

a. power because the engine takes in less air.

b. thrust because the propeller is less efficient in thin air.

c. lift because thin air exerts less force on airfoils.

2. What is the standard atmosphere at sea level? (FAA-H-8083-25)

Standard atmosphere at sea level includes a surface temperature of 59°F or 15°C, and a surface pressure of 29.92 in. Hg or 1013.2 millibars.

3. What are standard atmosphere temperature and pressure lapse rates? (FAA-H-8083-25)

A temperature lapse rate is one in which the temperature decreases at the rate of approximately 3.5°F or 2°C per 1,000 feet up to 36,000 feet. Above this point, the temperature is considered constant up to 80,000 feet. A standard pressure lapse rate is one in which pressure decreases at a rate of approximately 1 in. Hg per 1,000 feet of altitude gain to 10,000 feet.

4. Define the term "pressure altitude." (FAA-H-8083-25)

Pressure altitude is the height above a standard datum plane. An altimeter is a sensitive barometer calibrated to indicate altitude in the standard atmosphere. If the altimeter is set for 29.92 in. Hg Standard Datum Plane (SDP), the altitude indicated is the pressure altitude—the altitude in the standard atmosphere corresponding to the sensed pressure.

5. Why is pressure altitude important? (FAA-H-8083-25)

Pressure altitude is important as a basis for determining airplane performance as well as for assigning flight levels to airplanes operating above 18,000 feet.

6. What are two methods of determining pressure altitude? (FAA-H-8083-25)

Pressure altitude can be determined by either of two methods:

a. By setting the barometric scale of the altimeter to 29.92 and reading the indicated altitude, or

b. By applying a correction factor to the indicated altitude according to the reported "altimeter setting."

7. Define the term "density altitude." (FAA-H-8083-25)

Density altitude is pressure altitude corrected for nonstandard temperature. It is the altitude in the standard atmosphere corresponding to a particular value of air density.

8. How does air density affect aircraft performance? (FAA-H-8083-25)

As the density of the air increases (lower density altitude), airplane performance increases and conversely, as air density decreases (higher density altitude), airplane performance decreases. A decrease in air density means a high density altitude; an increase in air density means a lower density altitude.

9. How is density altitude determined? (FAA-H-8083-25)

First find pressure altitude and then correct it for nonstandard temperature variations. Because density varies directly with pressure, and inversely with temperature, a given pressure altitude may exist for a wide range of temperatures. However, a known density occurs for any one temperature and pressure altitude. Regardless of the actual altitude at which the airplane is operating, it will perform as though it were operating at an altitude equal to the existing density altitude.

10. **What factors affect air density?** (FAA-H-8083-25)

Air density is affected by changes in altitude, temperature, and humidity. High density altitude refers to thin air while low density altitude refers to dense air. The conditions that result in a high density altitude are high elevations, low atmospheric pressures, high temperatures, high humidity, or some combination of these factors. Lower elevations, high atmospheric pressure, low temperatures, and low humidity are more indicative of low density altitude.

11. **What effect does atmospheric pressure have on air density?** (FAA-H-8083-25)

Air density is directly proportional to pressure. If the pressure is doubled, the density is doubled, and if the pressure is lowered, so is the density. This statement is true only at a constant temperature.

12. **What effect does temperature have on air density?** (FAA-H-8083-25)

Increasing the temperature of a substance decreases its density. Conversely, decreasing the temperature increases the density. Thus, the density of air varies inversely with temperature. This statement is true only at a constant pressure.

13. **Since temperature and pressure decrease with altitude, how will air density be affected overall?** (FAA-H-8083-25)

The decrease in temperature and pressure have conflicting effects on density as you go up in altitude, but the fairly rapid drop in pressure with increasing altitude is usually the dominating factor. Hence, the density is likely to decrease with altitude gain.

14. **What effect does humidity have on air density?** (FAA-H-8083-25)

Water vapor is lighter than air, so moist air is lighter than dry air. As the water content of the air increases, the air becomes less dense, increasing density altitude and decreasing performance. It is lightest or least dense when it contains the maximum amount of water vapor. Humidity alone is usually not considered an important factor in calculating density altitude and airplane performance, but it does contribute.

15. What is the definition of the term "relative humidity"? (FAA-H-8083-25)

Relative humidity refers to the amount of water vapor in the atmosphere, and is expressed as a percentage of the maximum amount of water vapor the air can hold. This amount varies with the temperature—warm air can hold more water vapor and colder air can hold less.

16. What effect does landing at high-elevation airports have on ground speed with comparable conditions relative to temperature, wind and airplane weight? (FAA-H-8083-25)

Even if you use the same indicated airspeed appropriate for sea level operations, true airspeed is faster, resulting in a faster ground speed (with a given wind condition) throughout the approach, touchdown, and landing roll. This means greater distance to clear obstacles during the approach, a longer ground roll, and consequently the need for a longer runway. All of these factors should be taken into consideration when landing at high-elevation fields, particularly if the field is short.

B. Aircraft Performance

1. What are some of the main elements of aircraft performance? (FAA-H-8083-25)

a. Takeoff and landing distance

b. Rate-of-climb

c. Ceiling

d. Payload

e. Range

f. Speed

g. Maneuverability

h. Stability

i. Fuel economy

2. What is the relationship of lift, weight, thrust and drag in steady, unaccelerated, level flight? (FAA-H-8083-25)

For the airplane to remain in steady, level flight, equilibrium must be obtained by a lift equal to the airplane weight and powerplant thrust equal to the airplane drag.

3. What are the two types of drag? (FAA-H-8083-25)

Total drag may be divided into two parts: the wing drag (induced), and drag from everything but the wings (parasite).

4. Define induced drag. (FAA-H-8083-25)

Induced drag is the part of total drag created by the production of lift. Induced drag increases with a decrease in airspeed. The lower the airspeed, the greater the angle of attack required to produce lift equal to the airplane's weight, and therefore the greater the induced drag.

5. Define parasite drag. (FAA-H-8083-25)

Parasite drag is the part of total drag created by the form or shape of airplane parts. It is the sum of pressure and friction drag due to the airplane's basic configuration and is independent of lift. It is greatest at high airspeeds and is proportional to the square of the airspeed: if the airspeed were doubled, the parasite drag would be quadrupled.

6. How much will drag increase as airplane speed increases? (FAA-H-8083-25)

If an airplane in a steady flight condition at 100 knots is then accelerated to 200 knots, the parasite drag becomes four times as great, but the power required to overcome that drag is eight times the original value. Conversely, when the airplane is operated in steady, level flight at twice as great a speed, the induced drag is one-fourth the original value, and the power required to overcome that drag is only one-half the original value.

7. **Discuss the relationship of thrust and power as it relates to airplane climb performance.** (FAA-H-8083-25)

    Climb depends upon the reserve power or thrust. Reserve power is the available power over and above that required to maintain horizontal flight at a given speed. Thus, if an airplane is equipped with an engine that produces 200 total available horsepower and the airplane requires only 130 horsepower at a certain level flight speed, the power available for climb is 70 horsepower.

8. **Define the term "service ceiling."** (FAA-H-8083-25)

    Service ceiling is the maximum density altitude where the best rate-of-climb airspeed will produce a 100 feet-per-minute climb at maximum weight while in a clean configuration with maximum continuous power.

9. **Will an aircraft always be capable of climbing to and maintaining its service ceiling?** (FAA-H-8083-25)

    No. Depending on the density altitude, an airplane may not be able to reach it published service ceiling on any given day.

10. **What is the definition of "absolute ceiling"?** (FAA-H-8083-25)

    Absolute ceiling is the altitude at which a climb is no longer possible.

11. **What is meant by the terms "power loading" and "wing loading"?** (FAA-H-8083-25)

    Power loading is expressed in pounds per horsepower and is obtained by dividing the total weight of the airplane by the rated horsepower of the engine. It is a significant factor in the airplane's takeoff and climb capabilities.

    Wing loading is expressed in pounds per square foot and is obtained by dividing the total weight of the airplane in pounds by the wing area (including ailerons) in square feet. It is the airplane's wing loading that determines the landing speed.

12. Define the terms "maximum range" and "maximum endurance." (FAA-H-8083-25)

Maximum range is the maximum distance an airplane can fly for a given fuel supply and is obtained at the maximum lift/drag ratio (L/D_{MAX}). For a given airplane configuration, the maximum lift/drag ratio occurs at a particular angle of attack and lift coefficient, and is unaffected by weight or altitude.

Maximum endurance is the maximum amount of time an airplane can fly for a given fuel supply and is obtained at the point of minimum power required since this would require the lowest fuel flow to keep the airplane in steady, level flight.

13. What is ground effect? (FAA-H-8083-25)

Ground effect occurs due to the interference of the ground surface with the flow pattern about the airplane in flight, when the airplane is flown at approximately one wingspan above the surface. Especially with low-wing aircraft, it is most significant when the airplane is maintaining a constant attitude at low airspeed and low altitude. For example: during landing flare before touchdown, and during takeoff when the airplane lifts off and accelerates to climb speed. A wing in ground effect has a reduction in upwash, downwash, and tip vortices. With reduced tip vortices, induced drag is reduced. When the wing is at a height equal to one-fourth the span, the reduction in induced drag is about 25 percent, and when the wing is at a height equal to one-tenth the span, this reduction is about 50 percent.

14. What major problems can be caused by ground effect? (FAA-H-8083-25)

During landing—At a height of approximately one-tenth of a wing span above the surface, drag may be 50 percent less than when the airplane is operating out of ground effect. Therefore, any excess speed during the landing phase may result in a significant float distance. In such cases, if care is not exercised by the pilot, he/she may run out of runway and options at the same time.

Continued...

During takeoff—Due to the reduced drag in ground effect, the aircraft may seem capable of takeoff well below the recommended speed. However, as the airplane rises out of ground effect with a deficiency of speed, the greater induced drag may result in very marginal climb performance, or the inability of the airplane to fly at all. In extreme conditions such as high gross weight and high density altitude, the airplane may become airborne initially with a deficiency of speed and then settle back to the runway.

15. What does "flight in the region of normal command" mean? (FAA-H-8083-25)

It means that while holding a constant altitude, a higher airspeed requires a higher power setting, and a lower airspeed requires a lower power setting. The majority of all airplane flying (climb, cruise, and maneuvers) is conducted in the region of normal command.

16. What does "flight in the region of reversed command" mean? (FAA-H-8083-25)

It means that a higher airspeed requires a lower power setting, and a lower airspeed requires a higher power setting to hold altitude. It does not imply that a decrease in power will produce lower airspeed. The region of reversed command is encountered in the low-speed phases of flight. Flight speeds below the speed for maximum endurance (lowest point on the power curve) require higher power settings with a decrease in airspeed. Because the need to increase the required power setting with decreased speed is contrary to the "normal command" of flight, flight speeds between minimum required power setting (speed) and the stall speed (or minimum control speed) is termed the *region of reversed command*. In the region of reversed command, a decrease in airspeed must be accompanied by an increased power setting in order to maintain steady flight.

17. What are examples of where an airplane would be operating in the region of reversed command? (FAA-H-8083-25)

a. An airplane performing a low airspeed, high-pitch attitude, powered approach for a short-field landing.

b. A soft-field takeoff and climb where the pilot attempts to climb out of ground effect without first attaining normal climb pitch attitude and airspeed, is an example of inadvertently operating in the region of reversed command at a dangerously low altitude.

18. Explain how runway surface and gradient affect performance. (FAA-H-8083-25)

a. *Runway surface* — Any surface that is not hard and smooth will increase the ground roll during takeoff. This is due to the inability of the tires to smoothly roll along the runway. Although muddy and wet surface conditions can reduce friction between the runway and the tires, they can also act as obstructions and reduce the landing distance.

b. *Braking effectiveness* — The amount of power that is applied to the brakes without skidding the tires is referred to as braking effectiveness. Ensure that runways are adequate in length for takeoff acceleration and landing deceleration when less than ideal surface conditions are being reported, as it affects braking ability.

c. *Runway gradient or slope* — A positive gradient indicates that the runway height increases, and a negative gradient indicates that the runway decreases in height. An upsloping runway impedes acceleration and results in a longer ground run during takeoff. However, landing on an upsloping runway typically reduces the landing roll. A downsloping runway aids in acceleration on takeoff resulting in shorter takeoff distances. The opposite is true when landing, as landing on a downsloping runway increases landing distances.

19. What factors affect the performance of an aircraft during takeoffs and landings? (FAA-H-8083-25)

a. Air density (density altitude)

b. Surface wind

c. Runway surface

d. Upslope or downslope of runway

e. Weight

f. Powerplant thrust

20. What effect does wind have on aircraft performance? (FAA-H-8083-25)

Takeoff—A headwind increases airplane performance by shortening the takeoff distance and increasing the angle of climb. However, a tailwind decreases performance by increasing the takeoff distance and reducing the angle of climb. The pilot must carefully consider the decrease in airplane performance before attempting a downwind takeoff.

Landing—A headwind increases airplane performance by steepening the approach angle and reducing the landing distance. A tailwind decreases performance by decreasing the approach angle and increasing the landing distance. Again, the pilot must take the wind into consideration prior to landing.

Cruise flight—Winds aloft have a somewhat opposite effect; a headwind decreases performance by reducing ground speed, which in turn increases the fuel requirement for the flight. A tailwind increases performance by increasing the ground speed, which in turn reduces the fuel required for the flight.

21. How does weight affect takeoff and landing performance? (FAA-H-8083-25)

Increased gross weight can produce these effects:

a. Higher liftoff and landing speed required;

b. Greater mass to accelerate or decelerate (slow acceleration/deceleration);

c. Increased retarding force (drag and ground friction); and

d. Longer takeoff and ground roll.

The effect of gross weight on landing distance is that the airplane will require a greater speed to support the airplane at the landing angle of attack and lift coefficient resulting in an increased landing distance.

22. What effect does an increase in density altitude have on takeoff and landing performance? (FAA-H-8083-25)

An increase in density altitude results in:

a. Increased takeoff distance (greater takeoff TAS required).

b. Reduced rate of climb (decreased thrust and reduced acceleration).

c. Increased true airspeed on approach and landing (same IAS).

d. Increased landing roll distance.

An increase in density altitude (decrease in air density) will increase the landing speed but will not alter the net retarding force. Thus, the airplane will land at the same indicated airspeed as normal but because of reduced air density the true airspeed will be greater. This will result in a longer minimum landing distance.

23. Why does the manufacturer provide various manifold pressure/prop settings for a given power output?

The various power MAP/rpm combinations are provided so the pilot has a choice between operating the aircraft at best efficiency (minimum fuel flow) or operating at best power/speed condition. An aircraft engine operated at higher rpms will produce more friction and, as a result, use more fuel. On the other hand, an aircraft operating at higher and higher altitudes will not be able to continue to produce the same constant power output due to a drop in manifold pressure. The only way to compensate for this is by operating the engine at a higher rpm.

24. What does the term 75% brake horsepower mean? (FAA-H-8083-25)

Brake horsepower (BHP) is the power delivered at the propeller shaft (main drive or main output) of an aircraft engine. 75% BHP means you are delivering 75 percent of the normally rated power or maximum continuous power available at sea level on a standard day to the propeller shaft.

25. Explain how 75% BHP can be obtained from your engine. (FAA-H-8083-25)

Set the throttle (manifold pressure) and propeller (rpm) to the recommended values found in the cruise performance chart of your POH.

26. When would a pilot lean a normally-aspirated direct-drive engine? (FAA-P-8740-13)

a. Lean anytime the power setting is 75 percent or less at any altitude.

b. At high-altitude airports, lean for taxi, takeoff, traffic pattern entry and landing.

c. When the density altitude is high (Hot, High, Humid).

d. For landings at airports below 5,000 feet density altitude, adjust the mixture for descent, but only as required.

e. Always consult the POH for proper leaning procedures.

27. What are the different methods available for leaning aircraft engines? (FAA-P-8740-13)

Tachometer Method—For best economy operation, the mixture is first leaned from full rich to maximum power (peak rpm), then the leaning process is slowly continued until the engine starts to run rough. Then, enrich the mixture sufficiently to obtain a smoothly firing engine.

Fuel Flowmeter Method—Aircraft equipped with fuel flowmeters require that you lean the mixture to the published (POH) or marked fuel flow to achieve the correct mixture.

Exhaust Gas Temperature Method—Lean the mixture slowly to establish peak EGT then enrich the mixture by 50° rich (cooler) of peak EGT. This will provide the recommended lean condition for the established power setting.

28. Define the following airplane performance speeds.
(FAA-H-8083-25)

V_{S0}—The calibrated power-off stalling speed or the minimum steady flight speed at which the airplane is controllable in the landing configuration.

V_{S1}—The calibrated power-off stalling speed or the minimum steady flight speed at which the airplane is controllable in a specified configuration.

V_Y—The calibrated airspeed at which the airplane will obtain the maximum increase in altitude per unit of time. This best rate-of-climb speed normally decreases slightly with altitude.

V_X—The calibrated airspeed at which the airplane will obtain the highest altitude in a given horizontal distance. This best angle-of-climb speed normally increases slightly with altitude.

V_{LE}—The maximum calibrated airspeed at which the airplane can be safely flown with the landing gear extended. This is a problem involving stability and controllability.

V_{LO}—The maximum calibrated airspeed at which the landing gear can be safely extended or retracted. This is a problem involving the air loads imposed on the operating mechanism during extension or retraction of the gear.

V_{FE}—The highest calibrated airspeed permissible with the wing flaps in a prescribed extended position. This is because of the air loads imposed on the structure of the flaps.

V_A—The calibrated design maneuvering airspeed. This is the maximum speed at which the limit load can be imposed (either by gusts or full deflection of the control surfaces) without causing structural damage.

V_{NO}—The maximum calibrated airspeed for normal operation or the maximum structural cruising speed. This is the speed at which exceeding the limit load factor may cause permanent deformation of the airplane structure.

V_{NE}—The calibrated airspeed which should *never* be exceeded. If flight is attempted above this speed, structural damage or structural failure may result.

29. The following questions are designed to provide you with a review of some of the basic information you should know about your specific airplane before taking a flight check or review.

a. What is the normal climb-out speed?

b. What is the best rate-of-climb speed?

c. What is the best angle-of-climb speed?

d. What is the maximum flap extension speed?

e. What is the maximum gear extension speed?

f. What is the maximum gear retraction speed?

g. What is the stall speed in the normal landing configuration?

h. What is the stall speed in the clean configuration?

i. What is the normal approach-to-land speed?

j. What is the maneuvering speed?

k. What is the red-line speed?

l. What speed will give you the best glide ratio?

m. What is the maximum window-open speed?

n. What is the maximum allowable crosswind component for the aircraft?

o. What takeoff distance is required if a takeoff were made from a sea level pressure altitude?

C. Aircraft Performance Charts

The following are typical questions concerning aircraft performance charts. Refer to your Pilot's Operating Handbook for the answers.

1. Takeoff and Landing Distance Charts

a. Given the following conditions:

Pressure Altitude = 4,000 feet
Temperature = 40°F
Runway = Hard Surfaced
Weight = Maximum Takeoff Weight
Wind = 10 Knot Headwind

What is the distance for a normal takeoff ground roll?

What is the distance to clear a 50-foot obstacle?

b. Given the following conditions:

Pressure altitude = 2,000 feet
Temperature = 25°C
Runway = Hard surfaced
Weight = Maximum Landing Weight
Wind = Calm

What is the normal landing distance?

What is the minimum landing distance over a 50-foot obstacle?

2. Time, Fuel, and Distance-to-Climb Chart

a. Given the following conditions:

Climb = 2,000 feet to 7,000 feet pressure altitude
Temperature = Standard
Airspeed = Best Rate-of-Climb
Wind speed = Calm

How much time is required for the climb?

How much fuel is required for the climb?

What distance will be covered during the climb?

3. Maximum Rate-of-Climb Chart

   a. Given the following conditions:

      Pressure Altitude = 4,000 feet
      Outside Air Temperature = 0°C

   What is the best rate-of-climb airspeed?

   What is the best rate-of-climb, in feet per minute?

4. Cruise Performance Chart

   a. Given the following conditions:

      Pressure Altitude = 6,000 feet
      Engine rpm = 2,400
      MAP = 22 inches
      Temperature = Standard

   What will the true airspeed be?

   What will the fuel consumption rate be?

   What will the percent brake horsepower be?

   b. Given the following conditions:

      Density Altitude at cruising altitude = 4,000 feet
      Temperature = Standard

   What percentage of brake horsepower will be required to produce the maximum true airspeed?

   What will the required power setting be?

5. Maximum Range/Endurance Chart

   a. Given the following conditions:

      Density Altitude = 8,000 feet
      Temperature = Standard
      Weight = Maximum Gross
      Wind = Calm
      Power = 75%
      BHP Fuel = Full Tanks (Standard) 45 minute reserve

   What true airspeed can be expected?

   What maximum range will be achieved?

   b. Using the data from the previous question, how long can the aircraft fly in hours?

6. Miscellaneous

a. Determine the approximate CAS you should use to obtain 180 knots TAS with a pressure altitude of 8,000 feet and a temperature of +4°C.

158 knots.

b. At speeds below 200 knots (where compressibility is not a factor), how is true airspeed computed?

True airspeed can be found by correcting calibrated airspeed for pressure altitude and temperature.

c. Compute the density altitude for the following conditions:

Temperature   = 20°C

Field Elevation   = 4,000 feet

Altimeter setting = 29.98

d. Compute the standard temperature at 9,000 feet.

The standard temperature at sea level is 15°C. The average lapse rate is 2° per 1,000 feet. Compute standard temperature by multiplying the altitude by 2 and then subtracting that number from 15. Based on this information,

$$15° - (2° \times 9 = 18°) = -3°C$$

The standard temperature at 9,000 feet is -3°C.

e. A descent is planned from 8,500 feet MSL when 20 NM from your destination airport. If ground speed is 150 knots and you desire to be at 4,500 feet MSL when over the airport, what should the rate of descent be?

- Change in altitude = 4,000 feet
- Calculate time to go 20 NM at 150 knots (8 minutes)
- 4,000 feet ÷ 8 minutes = 500 FPM

f. A descent is planned from 11,500 feet MSL to arrive at 7,000 feet MSL, 5 SM from a VORTAC. With a ground speed of 160 mph and a rate of descent of 600 FPM, at what distance from the VORTAC should the descent be started?

- Change in altitude = 4,500 feet
- Rate of Descent = 600 FPM
- Time to descend = 4,500 ÷ 600 = 7.5 minutes
- Ground speed in miles per minute = 160 ÷ 60 = 2.67 MPM
- 7.5 x 2.67 = 20 miles + 5 miles = 25 miles out

g. If fuel consumption is 15.3 GPH and ground speed is 167 knots, how much fuel is required for an aircraft to travel 620 NM?

- 620 nautical miles ÷ 167 knots = 221 minutes or 3 hours and 41 minutes
- 15.3 GPH x 3 hrs. 41 min. = 57 gallons of fuel used

h. If the ground speed is 215 knots, how far will the aircraft travel in 3 minutes?

- 215 knots ÷ 60 = 3.58 nautical miles per minute
- 3.58 NMPM x 3 minutes = 10.75 nautical miles

i. How accurate should you consider the predictions of performance charts to be?

Flight tests from which performance data was obtained were flown with a new, clean airplane, correctly rigged and loaded, and with an engine capable of delivering its full rated power. You can expect to do as well only if your airplane, too, is kept in peak condition.

D. Weight and Balance

1. What performance characteristics will be adversely affected when an aircraft has been overloaded? (FAA-H-8083-25)

a. Higher takeoff speed.

b. Longer takeoff run.

c. Reduced rate and angle of climb.

d. Lower maximum altitude.

e. Shorter range.

f. Reduced cruising speed.

g. Reduced maneuverability.

h. Higher stalling speed.

i. Higher landing speed.

j. Longer landing roll.

k. Excessive weight on the nosewheel.

2. If the weight and balance of an aircraft has changed due to the addition or removal of fixed equipment in the aircraft, what responsibility does the owner or operator have?

The owner or operator of the aircraft should ensure that maintenance personnel make appropriate entries in the aircraft records when repairs or modifications have been accomplished. Weight changes must be accounted for and proper notations made in weight and balance records. The appropriate form for these changes is "Major Repairs and Alterations" (FAA Form 337).

3. Define the term "center of gravity." (FAA-H-8083-25)

The center of gravity (CG) is the point about which an aircraft would balance if it were possible to support the aircraft at that point. It is the mass center of the aircraft, or the theoretical point at which the entire weight of the aircraft is assumed to be concentrated. The CG must be within specific limits for safe flight.

4. **What effect does a forward center of gravity have on an aircraft's flight characteristics?** (FAA-H-8083-25)

Higher stall speed—Stalling angle of attack reached at a higher speed due to increased wing loading.

Slower cruise speed—Increased drag, greater angle of attack required to maintain altitude.

More stable—The center of gravity is further forward from the center of pressure, which increases longitudinal stability.

Greater back elevator pressure required—Longer takeoff roll, higher approach speeds and problems with the landing flare.

5. **What effect does an aft center of gravity have on an aircraft's flight characteristics?** (FAA-H-8083-25)

Lower stall speed—Less wing loading.

Higher cruise speed—Reduced drag, smaller angle of attack required to maintain altitude.

Less stable—Stall and spin recovery more difficult; when angle of attack is increased it tends to result in additional increased angle of attack.

6. Define the following:

**Arm • Basic empty weight (GAMA) • Basic operating
weight • Center of gravity • Center of gravity limits •
Center of gravity range • Datum • Empty weight • Floor
load limit • Licensed empty weight • Fuel load • LEMAC •
Maximum allowable zero fuel weight • Maximum landing
weight • Maximum Ramp Weight • Maximum takeoff
weight • Maximum weight • Maximum zero fuel weight
(GAMA) • Mean aerodynamic chord • Moment •
Moment index • Payload (GAMA) • Ramp or taxi weight •
Standard empty weight (GAMA) • Station • Useful load**
(FAA-H-8083-25)

Arm—The horizontal distance in inches from the reference datum
line to the center of gravity of an item.

Basic empty weight (GAMA)—The standard empty weight plus
optional and special equipment that has been installed.

Basic operating weight—The weight of the aircraft, including the
crew, ready for flight but without payload and fuel. This term is
only applicable to transport aircraft.

Center of gravity—The point about which an aircraft would balance if it were possible to suspend it at that point, expressed in
inches from datum.

Center of gravity limits—The specified forward and aft or lateral
points beyond which the CG must not be located during takeoff,
flight or landing.

Center of gravity range—The distance between the forward and
aft CG limits indicated on pertinent aircraft specifications.

Datum—An imaginary vertical plane or line from which all mea-
surements of arm are taken. It is established by the manufacturer.

Empty weight—The airframe, engines, and all items of operating
equipment that have fixed locations and are permanently installed
in the aircraft. It includes optional and special equipment, fixed
ballast, hydraulic fluid, unusable fuel, and undrainable oil.

Floor load limit—The maximum weight the floor can sustain per square inch/foot as provided by the manufacturer.

Fuel load—The expendable part of the load of the aircraft. It includes only usable fuel, not fuel required to fill the lines or that which remains trapped in the tank sumps.

LEMAC—The leading edge of the mean aerodynamic chord.

Licensed empty weight—The empty weight that consists of the airframe, engine(s), unusable fuel, and undrainable oil plus standard and optional equipment as specified in the equipment list. Some manufacturers used this term prior to GAMA standardization.

Maximum allowable zero fuel weight—The maximum weight authorized for the aircraft not including fuel load. Zero fuel weight for each particular flight is the operating weight plus the payload.

Maximum landing weight—The maximum weight at which the aircraft may normally be landed. The maximum landing weight may be limited to a lesser weight when runway length or atmospheric conditions are adverse.

Maximum ramp weight—The total weight of a loaded aircraft, and includes all fuel. It is greater than the takeoff weight due to the fuel that will be burned during the taxi and runup operations. Ramp weight may also be referred to as taxi weight.

Maximum takeoff weight—The maximum allowable weight at the start of the takeoff run. Some aircraft are approved for loading to a greater weight (ramp or taxi) only to allow for fuel burnoff during ground operation. The takeoff weight for a particular flight may be limited to a lesser weight when runway length, atmospheric conditions, or other variables are adverse.

Maximum weight—The maximum authorized weight of the aircraft and all of its equipment as specified in the Type Certificate Data Sheets (TCDS) for the aircraft.

Maximum zero fuel weight (GAMA)—The maximum weight, exclusive of usable fuel.

Continued...

Mean aerodynamic chord (MAC)—The average distance from the leading edge to the trailing edge of the wing. The MAC is specified for the aircraft by determining the average chord of an imaginary wing which has the same aerodynamic characteristics as the actual wing.

Moment—The product of the weight of an item multiplied by its arm. Moments are expressed in pound-inches.

Moment index—A moment divided by a constant such as 100, 1,000, or 10,000. The purpose of using a moment index is to simplify weight and balance computations of large aircraft where heavy items and long arms result in large, unmanageable numbers.

Payload (GAMA)—The weight of occupants, cargo, and baggage.

Ramp or taxi weight—The maximum takeoff gross weight plus fuel to be burned during taxi and runup.

Standard empty weight (GAMA)—The airframe, engines, and all items of operating equipment that have fixed locations and are permanently installed in the airplane; including fixed ballast, hydraulic fluid, unusable fuel, and full engine oil.

Station—A location in the aircraft which is identified by a number designating its distance in inches from the datum. The datum is, therefore, identified as station zero. The station and arm are usually identical. An item located at station +50 would have an arm of 50 inches.

Useful load—The weight of the pilot, copilot, passengers, baggage, usable fuel and drainable oil. It is the empty weight subtracted from the maximum allowable takeoff weight. The term applies to general aviation aircraft only.

7. **What basic equation is used in all weight and balance problems to find the center of gravity location of an airplane and/or its components?** (FAA-H-8083-25)

Weight x Arm = Moment

By rearrangement of this equation to the forms,

Weight = Moment ÷ arm.

Arm = Moment ÷ weight.

CG = Moment ÷ weight.

With any two known values, the third value can be found.

8. **What basic equation is used to determine center of gravity?** (FAA-H-8083-25)

Center of gravity is determined by dividing total moments by total weight.

9. **Explain the term percent of mean aerodynamic chord (MAC).** (FAA-H-8083-1)

Expression of the CG relative to the MAC is a common practice in larger aircraft. The CG position is expressed as a percent MAC (percent of mean aerodynamic chord), and the CG limits are expressed in the same manner. Normally, an aircraft will have acceptable flight characteristics if the CG is located somewhere near the 25% average chord point. This means the CG is located one-fourth of the total distance back from the leading edge of the average wing section.

10. **If the weight of an aircraft is within takeoff limits but the CG limit has been exceeded, what actions can the pilot take to correct the situation?** (FAA-H-8083-25)

The most satisfactory solution to this type of problem is to shift baggage, passengers, or both in an effort to make the aircraft CG fall within limits.

11. When a shift in weight is required, what standardized and simple calculations can be made to determine the new CG? (FAA-H-8083-25)

A typical problem may involve calculation of a new CG for an aircraft which has shifted cargo due to the CG being out of limits.

Given:

Aircraft total weight .... 6,680 pounds
CG .... Station 80.0
CG limits .... Station 70-78

Find: What is the location of the CG if 200 pounds is shifted from the aft compartment at station 150 to the forward at station 30?

Solution:

a. $\dfrac{\text{Weight shifted x Distance moved}}{\text{Aircraft gross weight}}$ = CG change

b. $\dfrac{200 \times 120}{6,680}$ = 3.6 inches forward

c.
old CG	80.0 inches
minus change	−3.6
new CG	76.4 inches

This same formula may be used to calculate how much weight must be shifted when you know how far you want to move the CG to come within limits.

12. If the weight of an aircraft changes due to the addition or removal of cargo or passengers before flight, what formula may be used to calculate new CG? (FAA-H-8083-25)

A typical problem may involve the calculation of a new CG for an aircraft which, when loaded and ready for flight, receives some additional cargo or passengers just before departure time.

Given:

Aircraft total weight .... 6,860 pounds

CG .... Station 80.0

Find: What is the location of the CG if 140 lbs. of baggage is added to station 150?

Solution:

a. Use the added weight formula:

$$\frac{\text{Added weight (or removed)}}{\text{New total weight}} = \frac{\text{CG change}}{\text{Distance between weight \& old CG}}$$

$$\frac{140}{6,860 + 140} = \frac{\text{CG change}}{150 - 80}$$

$$\frac{140}{7,000} = \frac{\text{CG change}}{70}$$

CG change = 1.4 inches aft

b. Add the CG change to the old CG:

New CG = 80.0 in. + 1.4 in. = 81.4 in.

By using "old total weight and new CG," this same formula may be used to find out how much weight to add or remove, when it is known how far you want to move the CG to come within limits.

13. What simple and fundamental weight check can be made by all pilots before flight? (FAA-H-8083-25)

A useful load check can be made to determine if the useful load limit has been exceeded. This check may be a mental calculation if the pilot is familiar with the aircraft's limits and knows that unusually heavy loads are not aboard. The pilot needs to know the useful load limit of the particular aircraft. This information may be found in the latest weight and balance report, in a logbook, or on a Major Repair and Alteration Form located in the aircraft. If the useful load limit is not stated directly, simply subtract the empty weight from the maximum takeoff weight.

14. What factors would contribute to a change in center of gravity location during flight?

The operator's flight manual should show procedures which fully account for variations in CG travel during flight caused by variables such as the movement of passengers and the effect of the CG travel due to fuel used.

15. If actual weights for weight and balance computations are unknown, what weights may be assumed for weight and balance computations? (FAA-H-8083-1)

Some standard weights used in general aviation are:

Crew and Passengers .... 170 lbs./person
Gasoline .... 6 lbs./U.S. gal.
Oil .... 7.5 lbs./U.S. gal.
Water .... 8.35 lbs./U.S. gal.

Note: These weights are not to be used in lieu of available actual weights!

16. How is the CG affected during flight as fuel is used? (FAA-H-8083-25)

As fuel is burned during flight, the weight of the fuel tanks will change and as a result the CG will change. Most aircraft, however, are designed with the fuel tanks positioned close to the CG; therefore, the consumption of fuel does not affect the CG to any great extent. Also, the lateral balance can be upset by uneven fuel loading or burn-off. The position of the lateral CG is not normally computed for an airplane, but the pilot must be aware of the adverse effects that will result from a laterally unbalanced condition.

Weight and Balance Review

1. What is the center of gravity range for this aircraft at maximum takeoff weight?

2. What are the empty, basic, and maximum takeoff weights of your aircraft?

3. What is the maximum allowable weight for the baggage compartment?

4. How many people will this aircraft carry safely with a full fuel load?

5. What is your maximum allowable useful load?

6. Solve a weight and balance problem for the flight you plan to make with one FAA examiner on board. (Be sure to ask their actual weight!)

   a. Does your load fall within the weight and balance envelope?

   b. What is the final gross weight?

   c. How much fuel can be carried?

   d. How much baggage can be carried with full fuel?

7. Calculate the new CG for the above aircraft if an additional 80 pounds of baggage were loaded.

Additional Study Questions

1. What are three ways you can control lift during flight? (FAA-H-8083-25)

2. Define the term "best glide." When is it used? (FAA-H-8083-3)

3. Define the terms "endurance " and "range." (FAA-H-8083-25)

4. Performance chart data is based upon what type of runway surface? (FAA-H-8083-25)

5. The values for V_X and V_Y will be equal at what altitude? (FAA-H-8083-25)

6. What happens to V_X and V_Y as altitude is increased? (FAA-H-8083-25)

7. The performance data given for your aircraft is based upon what conditions? (FAA-H-8083-25)

8. During the enroute phase of flight, the CG moves aft due to fuel burn or a passenger moving. What effect will this have on various performance factors such as airspeed, stall speed, and range? (FAA-H-8083-25)

9. Discuss some of the other factors that will affect performance of an aircraft that are not included in the aircraft performance charts. (FAA-H-8083-25)

10. What is the principle factor that determines propeller efficiency? (FAA-H-8083-25)

Cross-Country
Flight Planning
and Procedures   **6**

A. Flight Plan

Be prepared to exhibit knowledge of the elements related to cross-country flight planning by presenting and explaining a pre-planned VFR cross-country flight, as previously assigned by the examiner. On the day of the test, the final flight plan shall include real-time weather to the first fuel stop. Computations shall be based on maximum allowable passenger, baggage and/or cargo loads.

The examiner will ask you to discuss the following:

1. Current and forecast weather at departure, en route, destination and alternate airports including:

a. METARs

b. Terminal forecasts

c. Area forecasts

d. Winds aloft forecasts

e. TWEB route forecasts

f. SIGMETs and AIRMETs

g. Pilot reports

2. Route selection including:

a. Selection of checkpoints

b. Selection of best altitude

c. Selection of alternate airport

3. Appropriate sectional charts:

a. Knowledge of chart symbols

b. Airspace

c. Communication frequencies

4. Current information on facilities and procedures:

a. NOTAMs

b. Special Notices

c. Services available at destination

d. Airport conditions including lighting, obstructions, and other notations in A/FD

5. Flight log:

a. Measurement of course (true and magnetic)

b. Distances between checkpoints and total

c. How true airspeed was obtained

d. Estimated ground speed

e. Total time en route

f. Amount of fuel required

6. Weight and balance:

a. Calculations for planned trip

b. Calculations for weight added or removed immediately before departure

B. Navigation

1. What is an RMI? (P/CG)

RMI is an abbreviation for radio magnetic indicator. It is an aircraft navigational instrument coupled with a gyro compass or similar compass that indicates the direction of a selected NAVAID (NDB or VOR) and indicates bearing with respect to the heading of the aircraft.

2. What is an HSI? (FAA-H-8083-15)

The HSI (horizontal situation indicator) is a flight navigation instrument that combines the heading indicator with a CDI, in order to provide the pilot with better situational awareness of location with respect to the courseline.

3. What is RNAV? (FAA-H-8083-15)

RNAV (area navigation) provides enhanced navigational capability
to the pilot, by computing the airplane position, actual track and
ground speed, then providing meaningful information relative to a
route of flight selected by the pilot. Typical RNAV equipment
provides the pilot with distance, time, bearing and crosstrack error
relative to the selected TO or "active" waypoint and the selected
route. Present day RNAV includes INS, LORAN, VOR/DME, and
GPS systems.

4. What is DME? (AIM 1-1-7)

Equipment (airborne and ground) used to measure, in nautical
miles, the slant range distance of an aircraft from the DME navigational aid. Aircraft equipped with DME are provided with distance
and groundspeed information when receiving a VORTAC or
TACAN facility. Operating frequency range of a DME according to
ICAO Annex 10 is from 960 MHz to 1215 MHz.

5. What is the effective range distance for DME? (AIM 1-1-7)

Operating on the line-of-sight principle, DME furnishes distance
information with a very high degree of accuracy. Reliable signals
may be received at distances up to 199 NM at line-of-sight altitude
with an accuracy of better than $\frac{1}{2}$ mile or 3 percent of the distance,
whichever is greater. Distance information received from DME
equipment is SLANT RANGE distance and not actual horizontal
distance.

6. Give a brief description of GPS. (AIM 1-1-19)

The Global Positioning System is a satellite-based radio navigation
system that broadcasts a signal used by receivers to determine
precise position anywhere in the world. The receiver tracks
multiple satellites and determines a pseudorange measurement that
is then used to determine the user location.

7. **Can handheld GPS receivers and GPS systems certified for VFR operations be used for IFR operations?** (AIM 1-1-19)

No, for the following reasons:

a. RAIM capability — VFR GPS receivers and all handheld units have no RAIM alerting capability. Loss of the required number of satellites in view, or the detection of a position error, cannot be displayed to the pilot by such receivers.

b. Database currency — In many receivers, an updatable database is used for navigation fixes, airports, and instrument procedures. These databases must be maintained to the current update for IFR operation, but no such requirement exists for VFR use.

c. Antenna location — In many VFR installations of GPS receivers, antenna location is more a matter of convenience than performance. In IFR installations, care is exercised to ensure that an adequate clear view is provided for the antenna to see satellites. If an alternate location is used, some portion of the aircraft may block the view of the antenna, causing a greater opportunity to lose navigation.

Note: VFR and handheld GPS systems are not authorized for IFR navigation, instrument approaches, or as a principal instrument flight reference. During IFR operations they may be considered only as an aid to situational awareness.

8. **Within which frequency band does the VOR equipment operate?** (AIM 1-1-3)

VHF band — 108.00 through 117.95 MHz

9. **What are the different methods for checking the accuracy of VOR equipment?** (14 CFR 91.171)

   a. VOT check; ±4°

   b. Ground checkpoint; ±4°

   c. Airborne checkpoint; ±6°

   d. Dual VOR check; 4° between each other

   e. Select a radial over a known ground point; ±6°

   A repair station can use a radiated test signal, but only the technician performing the test can make an entry in the logbook.

10. **What records must be kept concerning VOR checks?** (14 CFR 91.171)

    Each person making a VOR check shall enter the date, place, and bearing error and sign the aircraft log or other reliable record.

11. **Where can a pilot find the location of the nearest VOT testing stations?** (AIM 1-1-4)

    Locations of airborne check points, ground check points and VOTs are published in the A/FD and are depicted on the A/G voice communications panels on the NOS IFR area chart and IFR enroute low altitude chart.

12. **How may the course sensitivity be checked on a VOR receiver?** (FAA-H-8083-15)

    In addition to receiver tolerance checks required by regulations, course sensitivity may be checked by recording the number of degrees of change in the course selected as you rotate the OBS to move the CDI from center to the last dot on either side. This should be between 10° and 12°.

13. How can a pilot determine if a VOR or VORTAC has been taken out of service for maintenance? (AIM 1-1-12)

During periods of routine or emergency maintenance, coded identification (or code and voice, where applicable) is removed from certain FAA NAVAIDs. Removal of identification serves as a warning to pilots that the facility is officially off the air for tune-up or repair and may be unreliable even though intermittent or constant signals are received.

14. How do you find an ADF relative bearing?
(FAA-H-8083-15)

A relative bearing is the angular relationship between the aircraft heading and the station measured clockwise from the nose. The bearing is read directly on the ADF dial measured clockwise from zero.

15. How do you find an ADF magnetic bearing?
(FAA-H-8083-15)

A magnetic bearing is the direction of an imaginary line from the aircraft to the station or the station to the aircraft referenced to magnetic north. To determine, use this formula:

$$MH + RB = MB$$

(Magnetic Heading + Relative Bearing = Magnetic Bearing)

If the sum is more than 360, subtract 360 to get the magnetic bearing to the station. The reciprocal of this number is the magnetic bearing from the station.

16. What is ADF homing? (FAA-H-8083-15)

ADF homing is flying the aircraft on any heading required to keep the ADF needle on zero until the station is reached.

17. What is ADF tracking? (FAA-H-8083-15)

ADF tracking is a procedure used to fly a straight geographic flight path inbound to or outbound from an NDB. A heading is established that will maintain the desired track.

18. If a diversion to an alternate airport becomes necessary due to an emergency, what procedure should be used? (FAA-H-8083-25)

a. Consider relative distance to all suitable alternates;

b. Select the one most appropriate for the emergency at hand;

c. Determine magnetic course to alternate and divert immediately;

d. Wind correction, actual distance and estimated time/fuel can then be computed while enroute to alternate.

19. How can the course to an alternate be computed quickly? (FAA-H-8083-25)

Courses to alternates can be quickly measured by using a straight edge and the compass roses shown at VOR stations on the chart. VOR radials and airway courses (already oriented to magnetic direction) printed on the chart can be used to approximate magnetic bearings during VFR flights. Use the radial of a nearby VOR or airway that most closely parallels the course to the station. Distances can be determined by placing a finger at the appropriate place on a straight edge of a piece of paper and then measuring the approximate distance on the mileage scale at the bottom of the chart.

C. Airport and Traffic Pattern Operations

1. What recommended entry and departure procedures should be used at airports without an operating control tower? (AIM 4-3-3)

When entering a traffic pattern, enter the pattern in level flight, abeam the midpoint of the runway at pattern altitude. Maintain pattern altitude until abeam the approach end of the landing runway on the downwind leg. Complete the turn to final at least $\frac{1}{4}$ mile from the runway. When departing a traffic pattern, continue straight out, or exit with a 45-degree turn (to the left when in a left-hand traffic pattern; to the right when in a right-hand traffic pattern) beyond the departure end of the runway, after reaching pattern altitude.

2. What are the recommended traffic advisory practices at airports *without* an operating control tower? (AIM 4-1-9)

Pilots of inbound traffic should monitor and communicate as appropriate on the designated CTAF from 10 miles to landing. Pilots of departing aircraft should monitor/communicate on the appropriate frequency from start-up, during taxi, and until 10 miles from the airport unless federal regulations or local procedures require otherwise.

3. A large or turbine-powered aircraft is required to enter Class D airspace at what altitude? (14 CFR 91.129)

A large or turbine-powered airplane shall, unless otherwise required by the applicable distance-from-clouds criteria, enter the traffic pattern at an altitude of at least 1,500 feet above the elevation of the airport and maintain at least 1,500 feet until further descent is required for a safe landing.

4. If operating into an airport without an operating control tower which is located within the Class D airspace of an airport with an operating control tower, is it always necessary to communicate with the tower? (14 CFR 91.129)

Yes, operations to or from an airport in Class D airspace (airport traffic area) require communication with the tower even when operating to/from a satellite airport.

5. When conducting flight operations into an airport with an operating control tower, when should initial contact be established? (AIM 4-3-2)

When operating at an airport where traffic control is being exercised by a control tower, pilots are required to maintain two-way radio contact with the tower while operating within Class B, Class C, and Class D surface areas unless the tower authorizes otherwise. Initial call-up should be made about 15 miles from the airport.

6. **When departing a Class D surface area, what communication procedures are recommended?** (AIM 4-3-2)

   Unless there is good reason to leave the tower frequency before exiting the Class B, Class C and Class D surface areas, it is good operating practice to remain on the tower frequency for the purpose of receiving traffic information. In the interest of reducing tower frequency congestion, pilots are reminded that it is not necessary to request permission to leave the tower frequency once outside of Class B, Class C, and Class D surface areas.

7. **You discover that both the transmitter and receiver in your aircraft have become inoperative. What procedures should be used when attempting to enter a traffic pattern and land at a tower controlled airport?** (AIM 4-2-13)

   a. Remain outside or above Class D surface area.

   b. Determine direction and flow of traffic.

   c. Join the traffic pattern and wait for light gun signals.

   d. Daytime, acknowledge by rocking wings. Nighttime, acknowledge by flashing landing light or navigation lights.

8. **When a control tower located at an airport within Class D airspace ceases operation for the day, what happens to the lower limit of the controlled airspace?** (AIM 3-2-5)

   During the hours the tower is not in operation, Class E surface area rules or a combination of Class E rules down to 700 feet AGL and Class G rules to the surface will become applicable. Check the A/FD for specifics.

9. **If the rotating beacon is on at an airport during daylight hours, what significance does this have?** (AIM 2-1-8)

   In Class B, Class C, Class D, and Class E surface areas, operation of the airport beacon during the hours of daylight often indicates that the ground visibility is less than 3 miles and/or the ceiling is less than 1,000 feet. ATC clearance in accordance with Part 91 is required for landing, takeoff and flight in the traffic pattern. Pilots should not rely solely on the operation of the airport beacon to indicate if weather conditions are IFR or VFR. There is no regulatory requirement for daylight operation, and it is the pilot's responsibility to comply with proper preflight planning as required by 14 CFR Part 91.

10. **What are the various types of runway markings (precision instrument runway) and what do they consist of?** (AIM 2-3-3)

    a. *Runway designators*—Runway number is the whole number nearest one-tenth the magnetic azimuth of the centerline of the runway, measured clockwise from the magnetic north.

    b. *Runway centerline marking*—Identifies the center of the runway and provides alignment guidance during takeoff and landings; consists of a line of uniformly-spaced stripes and gaps.

    c. *Runway aiming point marking*—Serves as a visual aiming point for a landing aircraft; two rectangular markings consist of a broad white stripe located on each side of the runway centerline and approximately 1,000 feet from the landing threshold.

    d. *Runway touchdown zone markers*—Identify the touchdown zone for landing operations and are coded to provide distance information in 500 feet increments; groups of one, two, and three rectangular bars symmetrically arranged in pairs about the runway centerline.

    e. *Runway side stripe markings*—Delineate the edges of the runway and provide a visual contrast between runway and the abutting terrain or shoulders; continuous white stripes located on each side of the runway.

f. *Runway shoulder markings*—May be used to supplement runway side stripes to identify pavement areas contiguous to the runway sides that are not intended for use by aircraft; painted yellow.

g. *Runway threshold markings*—Used to help identify the beginning of the runway that is available for landing. Two configurations: either eight longitudinal stripes of uniform dimensions disposed symmetrically about the runway centerline, or the number of stripes is related to the runway width.

11. What are the various types of taxiway markings and what do they consist of? (AIM 2-3-4)

Markings for taxiways are yellow and consist of the following types:

a. *Taxiway centerline*—Single continuous yellow line; provides wingtip clearance when over center.

b. *Taxiway edge*—Used to define the edge of taxiway; two types, continuous and dashed.

c. *Taxiway shoulder*—Usually defined by taxiway edge markings; denotes pavement unusable for aircraft.

d. *Surface painted taxiway direction*—Yellow background with black inscription; supplements direction signs or when not possible to provide taxiway sign.

e. *Surface painted location signs*—Black background with yellow inscription; supplements location signs.

f. *Geographic position markings* —Located at points along low visibility taxi routes; used to identify aircraft during low visibility operations.

12. What are the six types of signs installed on airports? (AIM 2-3-7 through 2-3-13)

a. *Mandatory instruction signs*—Red background/white inscription; denotes hazardous areas.

b. *Location signs*—Black background/yellow inscription; used to identify either a taxiway or runway on which an aircraft is located.

c. *Direction signs*—Yellow background/black inscription; identifies designation(s) of intersecting taxiway(s) leading out of intersection that pilot would expect to turn onto or hold short of.

d. *Destination signs*—Yellow background/black inscription; signs have arrow showing direction of taxi route to that destination.

e. *Information signs*—Yellow background/black inscription; provide pilot information on such things as areas that cannot be seen by control tower, radio frequencies, noise abatement procedures, etc.

f. *Runway distance remaining signs*—Black background with white numeral inscription; indicates distance (in thousands of feet) of landing runway remaining.

13. The acronym LAHSO refers to what specific air traffic control procedure? (AIM 4-3-11)

"Land And Hold Short Operations." At controlled airports, air traffic control may clear a pilot to land and hold short of an intersecting runway, an intersecting taxiway, or some other designated point on a runway other than an intersecting runway or taxiway. Pilots may accept such a clearance provided that the pilot-in-command determines that the aircraft can safely land and stop within the Available Landing Distance (ALD). Student pilots or pilots not familiar with LAHSO should not participate in the program.

14. Where can Available Landing Distance (ALD) data be found? (AIM 4-3-11)

ALD data are published in the special notices section of the Airport/Facility Directory (A/FD) and in the U.S. Terminal Procedures Publications. Controllers will also provide ALD data upon request.

15. Where are runway incursions most likely to occur? (FAA-H-8083-25)

Runway incursions most likely to cause accidents generally occur at complex, high-volume airports where there are parallel/intersecting runways, multiple taxiway/runway intersections, complex taxi patterns, and/or the need for traffic to cross active runways. Data also shows that a disproportionately large number of runway incursions involve general aviation pilots and often result from misunderstood controller instructions, confusion, disorientation, and/or inattention. Nearly all are caused by human error.

16. What are several recommended practices in the prevention of runway incursions? (FAA-H-8083-25)

a. Read back all runway crossing and/or hold-short instructions.

b. Review airport layouts as part of preflight planning and before descending to land, and while taxiing as needed.

c. Know airport signage.

d. Review NOTAMs for information on runway/taxiway closures and construction areas.

e. Do not hesitate to request progressive taxi instructions from ATC when unsure of the taxi route.

f. Check for traffic before crossing any runway or entering a taxiway.

g. Turn on aircraft lights, and rotating beacon or strobe lights while taxing.

h. When landing, clear the active runway as quickly as possible; then wait for taxi instructions before further movement.

i. Study and use proper radio phraseology as described in the AIM in order to respond to and understand ground control instructions; and

j. Write down complex taxi instructions at unfamiliar airports.

17. Describe a displaced threshold. (AIM 2-3-3)

It is a threshold located at a point on the runway other than the designated beginning of the runway. Displacement of the threshold reduces the length of the runway available for landings. The portion of the runway behind it is available for takeoffs in either direction and landings from the opposite direction. A ten-foot-wide white threshold bar is located across the width of the runway at the displaced threshold. White arrows are located along the centerline in the area between the beginning of the runway and the displaced threshold. White arrowheads are located across the width of the runway just prior to the threshold bar.

18. Describe a tri-color light VASI system. (AIM 2-1-2)

A tri-color visual approach slope indicator (VASI) normally consists of a single light unit projecting a three-color visual approach path into the final approach area of the runway.

Red	Below glidepath
Amber	Above glidepath
Green	On glidepath

19. What is PAPI? (AIM 2-1-2)

The precision approach path indicator (PAPI) uses light units similar to the VASI but are installed in a single row of either two or four light units. These systems have an effective visual range of about 5 miles during the day and up to 20 miles at night. The row of light units is normally installed on the left side of the runway.

20. What is PVASI? (AIM 2-1-2)

Pulsating visual approach slope indicators normally consist of a single light unit projecting a two-color visual approach path into the final approach area of the runway upon which the indicator is installed. The useful range of the system is about four miles during the day and up to ten miles at night.

Pulsating white light	Above glidepath
Steady white light	On glidepath
Steady red light	Slightly below glidepath
Pulsating red light	Well below glidepath

D. 14 CFR Part 91

1. Can a commercial pilot allow a passenger to carry alcohol on board an aircraft for the purpose of consumption? (14 CFR 91.17)

No, the regulations do not specifically address this issue but do indicate that a person who is intoxicated (or becomes intoxicated) not be allowed on board an aircraft. Except in an emergency, no pilot of a civil aircraft may allow a person who appears to be intoxicated or who demonstrates by manner or physical indications that the individual is under the influence of drugs (except a medical patient under proper care) to be carried in that aircraft.

2. No person may act as a crewmember of a civil aircraft with a blood alcohol level of what value? (14 CFR 91.17)

No person may act or attempt to act as a crewmember of a civil aircraft while having .04% by weight or more alcohol in the blood.

3. When are the operation of portable electronic devices not allowed on board an aircraft? (14 CFR 91.21)

No person may operate, nor may any operator or pilot-in-command of an aircraft allow the operation of any portable electronic device on any of the following U.S.-registered aircraft:

a. Aircraft operated by a holder of an air carrier operator certificate or an operating certificate, or

b. Any other aircraft while it is operated under IFR.

4. Are there any exceptions allowed concerning portable electronic equipment on board aircraft? (14 CFR 91.21)

a. Portable voice recorders

b. Hearing aids

c. Heart pacemakers

d. Electric shavers

e. Any other portable electronic device that the operator of the aircraft has determined will not cause interference with the navigation or communication system of the aircraft on which it is to be used.

5. Preflight action as required by regulation for all flights away from the vicinity of the departure airport shall include a review of what specific information? (14 CFR 91.103)

For a flight under IFR or a flight not in the vicinity of an airport:

a. Weather reports and forecasts

b. Fuel requirements

c. Alternatives available if the planned flight cannot be completed

d. Any known traffic delays of which the pilot-in-command has been advised by ATC

e. Runway lengths of intended use

f. Takeoff and landing distance data

6. When are flight crewmembers required to wear their seatbelts? (14 CFR 91.105)

During takeoff and landing, and while en route, each required flight crewmember shall keep the safety belt fastened while at the crewmember station (also, during takeoff and landing only, the shoulder harness, if installed).

7. Is the use of safety belts and shoulder harnesses required when operating an aircraft on the ground? (14 CFR 91.107)

Yes; each person on board a U.S.-registered civil aircraft must occupy an approved seat or berth with a safety belt, and if installed, shoulder harness, properly secured about him or her during movement on the surface, takeoff and landing.

8. If a formation flight has been arranged in advance, can passengers be carried for hire? (14 CFR 91.111)

No; no person may operate an aircraft, carrying passengers for hire, in formation flight.

9. What is the maximum speed allowed when operating inside Class B airspace, under 10,000 feet and within a Class D surface area? (14 CFR 91.117)

Unless otherwise authorized or required by ATC, no person may operate an aircraft at or below 2,500 feet above the surface within 4 nautical miles of the primary airport of a Class C or Class D airspace area at an indicated airspeed of more than 200 knots. This restriction does not apply to operations conducted within a Class B airspace area. Such operations shall comply with the "below 10,000 feet MSL" restriction:

"No person shall operate an aircraft below 10,000 feet MSL, at an indicated airspeed of more than 250 knots."

10. What regulations pertain to altimeter setting procedures? (14 CFR 91.121)

Below 18,000 feet MSL:

a. The current reported altimeter setting of a station along the route and within 100 nautical miles of the aircraft.

b. If there is no station within the area described above, the current reported altimeter of an appropriate available station.

c. In the case of an aircraft not equipped with a radio, the elevation of the departure airport or an appropriate altimeter setting available before departure.

Note: If barometric pressure exceeds 31.00" Hg, set 31.00" (*see* AIM).

At or above 18,000 feet MSL set to 29.92" Hg.

11. What are the regulatory fuel requirements for both VFR and IFR flight (day and night)? (14 CFR 91.151, 91.167)

a. *VFR conditions:*

No person may begin a flight in an airplane under VFR conditions unless (considering wind and forecast weather conditions) there is enough fuel to fly to the first point of intended landing and, assuming normal cruising speed:

- During the day, to fly after that for at least 30 minutes; or
- At night, to fly after that for at least 45 minutes.

b. *IFR conditions:*

No person may operate a civil aircraft in IFR conditions unless it carries enough fuel (considering weather reports and forecasts) to:

- Complete the flight to the first airport of intended landing;
- Fly from that airport to the alternate airport; and
- Fly after that for 45 minutes at normal cruising speed.

If an alternate is not required, complete the flight to the destination airport with a 45-minute reserve remaining.

12. What minimum flight visibility and clearance from clouds are required for VFR flight in the following situations? (14 CFR 91.155)

Class C, D, or E Airspace (controlled airspace)

Less than 10,000 feet MSL:
Visibility: 3 statute miles
Cloud clearance: 500 feet below, 1,000 feet above, 2,000 feet horizontal

At or above 10,000 feet MSL:
Visibility: 5 statute miles
Cloud clearance: 1,000 feet below, 1,000 feet above, 1 statute mile horizontal

Class G Airspace (uncontrolled airspace)

1,200 feet or less above the surface (regardless of MSL altitude):

Day
> Visibility: 1 statute mile
> Cloud clearance: clear of clouds

Night
> Visibility: 3 statute miles
> Cloud clearance: 500 feet below, 1,000 feet above,
> 2,000 feet horizontal

More than 1,200 feet above the surface but less than 10,000 feet MSL:

Day
> Visibility: 1 statute mile
> Cloud clearance: 500 feet below, 1,000 feet above,
> 2,000 feet horizontal

Night
> Visibility: 3 statute miles
> Cloud clearance: 500 feet below, 1,000 feet above,
> 2,000 feet horizontal

More than 1,200 feet above the surface and at or above 10,000 feet MSL:

> Visibility: 5 statute miles
> Cloud clearance: 1,000 feet below, 1,000 feet above,
> 1 statute mile horizontal

13. When conducting IFR flight operations, what minimum altitudes are required over surrounding terrain?
(14 CFR 91.177)

If no applicable minimum altitudes apply:

a. Operations over an area designated as a mountainous area, an altitude of 2,000 feet above the highest obstacle within a horizontal distance of 4 nautical miles from the course to be flown; or

b. In any other case, an altitude of 1,000 feet above the highest obstacle within a horizontal distance of 4 nautical miles from the course to be flown.

14. What are several examples of situations in which an ELT is not required equipment on board the aircraft? (14 CFR 91.207)

Examples of operations where an ELT is not required are:

a. Ferrying aircraft for installation of an ELT

b. Ferrying aircraft for repair of an ELT

c. Aircraft engaged in training flights within a 50-nautical mile radius of an airport.

15. Where is altitude encoding transponder equipment required? (AIM 4-1-20)

In general, the regulations require aircraft to be equipped with Mode C transponders when operating:

a. At or above 10,000 feet MSL over the 48 contiguous states or the District of Columbia, excluding airspace below 2,500 feet AGL;

b. Within 30 miles of a Class B airspace primary airport, below 10,000 feet MSL;

c. Within and above all Class C airspace, up to 10,000 feet MSL;

d. Within 10 miles of certain designated airports, excluding airspace which is both outside the Class D surface area and below 1,200 feet AGL;

e. All aircraft flying into, within, or across the contiguous United States ADIZ.

16. Where are aerobatic flight maneuvers not permitted? (14 CFR 91.303)

No person may operate an aircraft in aerobatic flight—

a. Over any congested area of a city, town, or settlement;

b. Over an open air assembly of persons;

c. Within the lateral boundaries of the surface areas of Class B, Class C, Class D, or Class E airspace designated for an airport;

d. Within 4 nautical miles of the center line of any Federal airway;

e. Below an altitude of 1,500 feet above the surface; or

f. When flight visibility is less than 3 statute miles.

For the purposes of this section, aerobatic flight means an intentional maneuver involving an abrupt change in an aircraft's attitude, an abnormal attitude, or abnormal acceleration, not necessary for normal flight.

17. When must each occupant of an aircraft wear an approved parachute? (14 CFR 91.307)

a. Unless each occupant of the aircraft is wearing an approved parachute, no pilot of a civil aircraft carrying any person (other than a crewmember) may execute any intentional maneuver that exceeds:
   - A bank of 60° relative to the horizon; or
   - A nose-up or nose-down attitude of 30° relative to the horizon.

b. This regulation does not apply to:
   - Flight tests for pilot certification or rating; or
   - Spins and other flight maneuvers required by the regulations for any certificate or rating when given by a certified flight instructor or an Airline Transport Pilot.

18. What is required to operate an aircraft towing an advertising banner? (14 CFR 91.311)

No pilot of a civil aircraft may tow anything with that aircraft (other than under 91.309 "Towing gliders") except in accordance with the terms of a certificate of waiver issued by the Administrator.

19. What categories of aircraft cannot be used in the carriage of persons or property for hire? (14 CFR 91.313, 91.315, and 91.319)

a. Restricted category

b. Limited category

c. Experimental

E. AIM (Aeronautical Information Manual)

1. What is primary radar and secondary radar? (P/CG)

Primary radar—A radar system in which a minute portion of a
radio pulse transmitted from a site is reflected by an object and
then received back at that site for processing and display at an Air
Traffic Control facility.

Secondary radar—A radar system in which the object to be
detected is fitted with a transponder. Radar pulses transmitted from
the searching transmitter/receiver (interrogator) site are received in
the transponder and used to trigger a distinctive transmission from
the transponder. The reply transmission, rather than the reflected
signal, is then received back at the transmitter/receiver site for processing and display at an Air Traffic Control facility.

2. What is airport surveillance radar? (P/CG)

Airport surveillance radar (ASR) is approach control radar used to
detect and display an aircraft's position in the terminal area. ASR
provides range and azimuth information but does not provide elevation data. Coverage of ASR can extend up to 60 miles.

3. Describe the various types of terminal radar services available for VFR aircraft. (AIM 4-1-17)

Basic radar service—Safety alerts, traffic advisories, limited radar
vectoring (on a workload-permitting basis) and sequencing at
locations where procedures have been established for this purpose
and/or when covered by a letter of agreement.

TRSA service—Radar sequencing and separation service for
participating VFR aircraft in a TRSA.

Class C service—This service provides, in addition to basic radar
service, approved separation between IFR, and VFR aircraft, and
sequencing of VFR arrivals to the primary airport.

Class B service—Provides, in addition to basic radar service,
approved separation of aircraft based on IFR, VFR, and/or weight,
and sequencing of VFR arrivals to the primary airport(s).

4. What frequencies other than 121.5 are monitored by most FSS's? (AIM 4-2-14)

Frequencies are listed in the Airport/Facility Directory. 122.0 MHz is assigned as the Enroute Flight Advisory Service frequency at selected FSS's. Certain FSS's provide Local Airport Advisory on 123.6 MHz. If in doubt as to what frequency to use, 122.2 MHz is assigned to the majority of FSS's as a common enroute simplex frequency.

5. If operations are not being conducted in airspace requiring a transponder, can an aircraft equipped with a transponder leave it off? (AIM 4-1-20)

In all cases, while in controlled airspace (Class A, B, C, D, or E airspace) each pilot operating an aircraft equipped with an operable ATC transponder maintained in accordance with 14 CFR §91.413 shall operate the transponder, including Mode C if installed, on the appropriate code or as assigned by ATC. In Class G airspace (uncontrolled airspace), the transponder should be operating while airborne, unless otherwise requested by ATC.

6. At what altitude would a pilot expect to encounter military aircraft when navigating through a military training route designated "VR1207"? (AIM 3-5-2)

Less than 1,500 AGL; Military training routes with no segment above 1,500 feet AGL shall be identified by four-digit characters; e.g., IR1206, VR1207. MTRs that include one or more segments above 1,500 feet AGL shall be identified by three-digit characters; e.g., IR206, VR207.

7. What is a composite flight plan? (AIM 5-1-7)

Flight plans which specify VFR operations for one portion of the flight and IFR for another portion will be accepted by the FSS at the point of departure. If VFR flight is conducted for the first portion and IFR for the last portion:

a. The pilot should report the departure time to the FSS with which he filed his VFR/IFR flight plan;

b. At the point of intended change, close the VFR portion;

c. Request ATC clearance from the FSS nearest the point at which the change from VFR to IFR is proposed; and

d. Remain in VFR weather conditions until operating in accordance with the IFR clearance.

8. What is an "abbreviated" IFR flight plan? (P/CG)

An abbreviated IFR flight plan is an authorization by ATC requiring pilots to submit only that information needed for the purpose of ATC. It is frequently used by aircraft which are airborne and desire an instrument approach or by an aircraft on the ground which desires to climb to VFR-On-Top conditions.

9. How long will a flight plan remain on file after the proposed departure time has passed? (AIM 5-1-12)

To prevent computer saturation in the en route environment, parameters have been established to delete proposed departure flight plans which have not been activated. Most centers have this parameter set so as to delete these flight plans a minimum of 1 hour after the proposed departure time.

10. If you fail to report a change in arrival time or forget to close your flight plan, when will search and rescue procedures begin? (AIM 5-1-13)

If you fail to report or cancel your flight plan within $\frac{1}{2}$ hour after your ETA, search and rescue procedures are started.

11. What constitutes a change in flight plan? (AIM 5-1-11)

In addition to altitude or flight level, destination and/or route changes, increasing or decreasing the speed of the aircraft constitutes a change in flight plan. Therefore, anytime the average true airspeed at cruising altitude between reporting points varies or is expected to vary from that given in the flight plan by ±5 percent or 10 knots, whichever is greater, ATC should be advised.

12. What is a DVFR flight plan? (AIM 5-1-6)

Defense VFR; VFR flights into a coastal or domestic ADIZ/DEWIZ are required to file DVFR flight plans for security purposes. The flight plan must be filed before departure.

13. What is an ADIZ? (AIM 5-6-1)

In the interest of national security, all aircraft entering domestic U.S. airspace from points outside must provide for identification prior to entry. To facilitate early identification of all aircraft in the vicinity of U.S. and international airspace boundaries, Air Defense Identification Zones (ADIZs) have been established.

14. Where are Air Defense Identification Zones normally located? (AIM Glossary)

Domestic ADIZ—located within the United States along an international boundary of the United States.

Coastal ADIZ—located over the coastal waters of the United States.

Distant Early Warning Identification Zone (DEWIZ)—located over the coastal waters of the State of Alaska.

Land-based ADIZ—located over U.S. metropolitan areas, which is activated and deactivated as needed, with dimensions, activation dates and other relevant information disseminated via NOTAM.

15. What requirements must be satisfied prior to operations into, within or across an ADIZ? (AIM 5-6-1)

Operational requirements for aircraft operations associated with an ADIZ are as follows:

Flight plan—An IFR or DVFR flight plan must be filed with the appropriate aeronautical facility.

Two-way radio—An operating two-way radio is required.

Transponder—Aircraft must be equipped with an operable radar beacon transponder having altitude reporting (Mode C) capabilities. The transponder must be turned on and set to the assigned ATC code.

Position reports—For IFR flights, normal position reporting. For DVFR flights, an estimated time of ADIZ penetration must be filed at least 15 minutes prior to entry.

Aircraft position tolerances—Over land, a tolerance of ±5 minutes from the estimated time over a reporting point and within 10 NM from the centerline of an intended track over an estimated reporting point. Over water, a tolerance of ±5 minutes from the estimated time over a reporting point or point of penetration and within 20 NM from centerline of an intended track over an estimated reporting point.

16. Briefly describe the six classes of U.S. airspace.
(AIM 3-2-2 through 3-2-6, and 3-3-1)

Class A airspace—Generally, airspace from 18,000 feet MSL up to and including FL600, including airspace overlying the waters within 12 nautical miles of the coast of the 48 contiguous states and Alaska; and designated international airspace beyond 12 nautical miles of the coast of the 48 contiguous states and Alaska within areas of domestic radio navigational signal or ATC radar coverage, and within which domestic procedures are applied.

Class B airspace—Generally, airspace from the surface to 10,000 feet MSL surrounding the nation's busiest airports in terms of IFR operations or passenger enplanements. The configuration of each Class B airspace area is individually tailored and consists of a surface area and two or more layers, (some resemble upside-down wedding cakes), and is designated to contain all published instrument procedures once an aircraft enters the airspace. An ATC clearance is required for all aircraft to operate in the area, and all aircraft cleared as such receive separation services within the airspace. The cloud clearance requirement for VFR operations is "clear of clouds."

Class C airspace—Generally, airspace from the surface to 4,000 feet above the airport elevation (charted in MSL) surrounding airports that have an operational control tower, are serviced by a radar approach control, and that have a certain number of IFR operations or passenger enplanements. Although the configuration of each Class C airspace area is individually tailored, the airspace usually consists of a 5 NM radius core surface area that extends from the surface up to 4,000 feet above the airport elevation, and a 10 NM radius shelf area that extends from 1,200 feet to 4,000 feet above the airport elevation.

Class D airspace—Generally, airspace from the surface to 2,500 feet above the airport elevation (charted in MSL) surrounding airports that have an operational control tower. The configuration of each Class D airspace area is individually tailored and when instrument procedures are published, the airspace will normally be designed to contain those procedures.

Class E (controlled) airspace—Generally, if the airspace is not Class A, B, C, or D, and it is controlled airspace, it is Class E airspace. Class E airspace extends upward from either the surface or a designated altitude to the overlying or adjacent controlled airspace. Examples include: Surface areas designated for an airport, extensions to a surface area, airspace used for transition, enroute domestic areas, Federal airways, offshore airspace areas.

Class G (uncontrolled) airspace—Class G airspace is that portion of the airspace that has not been designated as Class A, B, C, D, and E airspace.

17. Define the following types of airspace.
(AIM 3-4-2 through 3-4-8; 3-5-7)

Prohibited Area—For security or other reasons, aircraft flight is prohibited.

Restricted Area—Contains unusual, often invisible hazards to aircraft, flights must have permission from the controlling agency, if VFR. IFR flights will be cleared through or vectored around it.

Military Operations Area—Designed to separate military training from IFR traffic. Permission is not required, but VFR flights should exercise caution. IFR flights will be cleared through or vectored around it.

Warning Area—Same hazards as a restricted area, it is established beyond the 3-mile limit of International Airspace. Permission is not required, but a flight plan is advised.

Alert Area—Airspace containing a high volume of pilot training or unusual aerial activity. No permission is required, but VFR flights should exercise caution. IFR flights will be cleared through or vectored around it.

Controlled Firing Areas—CFAs contain activities which, if not conducted in a controlled environment, could be hazardous to non-participating aircraft. The distinguishing feature of the CFA, as compared to other special use airspace, is that its activities are suspended immediately when spotter aircraft, radar or ground lookout positions indicate an aircraft might be approaching the area. CFAs are not charted.

National Security Areas—Airspace of defined vertical and lateral dimensions established at locations where there is a requirement for increased security and safety of ground facilities. Pilots are requested to voluntarily avoid flying through the depicted NSA. When it is necessary to provide a greater level of security and safety, flight in NSAs may be temporarily prohibited by regulation under the provisions of 14 CFR §99.7.

18. What is a temporary flight restrictions area and how would you know it exists? (14 CFR 91.145; AIM 3-5-3)

The FAA will issue a Notice to Airmen (NOTAM) designating an area of airspace in which a temporary flight restriction applies when it determines that one is necessary to protect persons or property on the surface or in the air, to maintain air safety and efficiency, or to prevent the unsafe congestion of aircraft in the vicinity of an aerial demonstration or major sporting event. Always check for appropriate NOTAMs during flight planning.

19. What is a TRSA? (P/CG)

A terminal radar service area (TRSA) consists of airspace surrounding designated airports wherein ATC provides radar vectoring, sequencing, and separation on a full time basis for all IFR and participating VFR aircraft. Pilot participation is urged but not mandatory.

20. What procedures should be used in avoiding wake turbulence when landing? (AIM 7-3-6)

a. Landing behind a larger aircraft, on the same runway: stay at or above the larger aircraft's final approach flight path. Note its touchdown point and land beyond it.

b. Landing behind a larger aircraft, on a parallel runway closer than 2,500 feet: consider possible drift to your runway. Stay at or above the larger aircraft's final approach flight path and note its touchdown point.

c. Landing behind a larger aircraft on a crossing runway: cross above the larger aircraft's flight path.

d. Landing behind a departing larger aircraft on the same runway: note the larger aircraft's rotation point, and land well before the rotation point.

e. Landing behind a departing larger aircraft on a crossing runway: note the larger aircraft's rotation point. If it is past the intersection, continue the approach, and land prior to the intersection. If the larger aircraft rotates prior to the intersection, avoid flight below the larger aircraft's flight path. Abandon the approach unless a landing is ensured well before reaching the intersection.

21. What procedures should be used in avoiding wake turbulence when taking off? (AIM 7-3-6)

a. Departing behind a larger aircraft: note the larger aircraft's rotation point, rotate prior to larger aircraft's rotation point. Continue climb above the larger aircraft's climb path until turning clear of its wake.

b. Intersection takeoffs on the same runway: be alert to adjacent larger aircraft operations, particularly upwind of your runway. If intersection takeoff clearance is received, avoid a subsequent heading which will cross below the larger aircraft's path.

c. Departing or landing after a larger aircraft executing a low approach, missed approach or touch-and-go landing: ensure that an interval of at least 2 minutes has elapsed before you take off or land. Because vortices settle and move laterally near the ground, the vortex hazard may continue to exist along the runway, particularly in light quartering wind situations.

d. Enroute VFR (thousand foot altitude plus 500 feet): avoid flight below and behind a large aircraft's path. If a larger aircraft is observed above or on the same track (meeting or overtaking), adjust your position laterally, preferably upwind.

22. Who is responsible for wake turbulence avoidance, the pilot or the air traffic controller? (AIM 7-3-8)

The pilot is responsible. Acceptance of instructions from ATC (traffic information, follow an aircraft, visual approach clearance), is acknowledgment that the pilot has accepted responsibility for his/her own wake turbulence separation.

23. Define the term hydroplaning. (FAA-H-8083-3)

Hydroplaning occurs when the tires are lifted off a runway surface by the combination of aircraft speed and a thin film of water present on the runway.

24. What are the three basic types of hydroplaning? (FAA-H-8083-3)

Dynamic—Occurs when there is standing water on the runway surface. Water about $\frac{1}{10}$-inch deep acts to lift the tire off the runway. The minimum speed at which dynamic hydroplaning occurs has been determined to be about 8.6 times the square root of the tire pressure in pounds per square inch.

Viscous—Occurs as a result of the viscous properties of water. A very thin film of fluid cannot be penetrated by the tire and the tire consequently rolls on top of the film. Viscous hydroplaning can occur at much slower speeds than dynamic hydroplaning but requires a smooth acting surface.

Reverted Rubber Hydroplaning—Occurs when a pilot, during the landing roll, locks the brakes for an extended period of time while on a wet runway. The friction creates heat which, combined with water, creates a steam layer between the aircraft tire and runway surface.

25. What is the best method of speed reduction if hydroplaning is experienced on landing? (FAA-H-8083-3)

Lowering the nosewheel on a wet runway of adequate length will reduce angle of attack and stabilize the airplane during rollout. Therefore it is important to have the nose tire tracking as soon as possible. Also, retracting the flaps as soon as possible will improve traction. This should be done with caution, however, especially if operating a retractable gear airplane. Above all, use good judgment and follow recommendations provided by the manufacturer.

26. What are several types of illusions in flight which may lead to errors in judgment on landing? (AIM 8-1-5)

Runway width illusion—Narrower than usual runway creates illusion aircraft is higher than actual; pilot tends to fly a lower approach than normal.

Runway and terrain slope illusion—Upsloping runway/terrain creates illusion aircraft is higher than actual; pilot tends to fly a lower approach than normal. Downsloping runway/terrain has the opposite effect.

Featureless terrain illusion—An absence of ground features creates illusion that aircraft is higher than actual; pilot tends to fly a lower approach than normal.

Atmospheric illusions—Rain on windscreen creates illusion of greater height; atmospheric haze creates illusion of greater distance from runway; pilot tends to fly a lower approach than normal.

27. What is the most effective method of scanning for other air traffic? (AIM 8-1-6)

Effective scanning is accomplished with a series of short, regularly spaced eye movements that bring successive areas of the sky into the central vision field. Each movement should not exceed 10°, and each area should be observed for at least 1 second to enable detection. Although horizontal back and forth eye movements seem preferred by most pilots, each pilot should develop a comfortable scanning pattern and then adhere to it to ensure optimum scanning.

28. Discuss recommended collision avoidance procedures and considerations in the following situations.
(FAA-H-8083-25)

a. *Before Takeoff*—Before taxiing onto a runway or landing area in preparation for takeoff, scan the approach area for possible landing traffic, executing appropriate maneuvers to provide a clear view of the approach areas.

b. *Climbs and Descents*—During climbs and descents in flight conditions that permit visual detection of other traffic, make gentle banks left and right at a frequency that allows continuous visual scanning of the airspace.

c. *Straight and Level*—During sustained periods of straight-and-level flight, execute appropriate clearing procedures at periodic intervals.

d. *Traffic Patterns*—Entries into traffic patterns while descending should be avoided.

e. *Traffic at VOR Sites*—Due to converging traffic, maintain sustained vigilance in the vicinity of VORs and intersections.

f. *Training Operations*—Maintain vigilance and make clearing turns before a practice maneuver. During instruction, the pilot should be asked to verbalize the clearing procedures (call out clear "left, right, above, below"). High-wing and low-wing aircraft have their respective blind spots: For high-wing aircraft, momentarily raise the wing in the direction of the intended turn and look for traffic prior to commencing the turn; for low-wing aircraft, momentarily lower the wing.

F. Night Flight Operations

1. Explain the arrangement and interpretation of the position lights on an aircraft. (FAA-H-8083-3)

A red light is located on the left wing tip, a green light is located on the right wing tip and a white light is located on the tail. If you see both a green and red light on another aircraft, then the other aircraft is generally approaching your position. If you only see a green light, then the other aircraft is moving left to right in relation to your position. If you only see a red light, then the aircraft is moving right to left in relation to your position.

2. Position lights are required to be on during what period of time? (14 CFR 91.209)

No person may operate an aircraft during the period from sunset to sunrise unless the aircraft has lighted position lights.

3. When operating an aircraft in, or in close proximity to, a night operations area, what is required of an aircraft? (14 CFR 91.209)

The aircraft must:
- Be clearly illuminated,
- Have position lights, or
- Be in an area marked by obstruction lights.

4. Are aircraft anticollision lights required to be on during night flight operations? (14 CFR 91.209)

Yes; however, if the pilot-in-command determines that because of operating conditions it would be in the interest of safety, the anti-collision lights can be turned off.

5. What are the different types of rotating beacons used to identify airports? (AIM 2-1-9)

a. White and green—lighted land airport

b. *Green alone—lighted land airport

c. White and yellow—lighted water airport

d. *Yellow alone—lighted water airport

e. Green, yellow, and white — lighted heliport

f. White (dual peaked) and green — military airport

Note: "Green alone" or "yellow alone" beacons are used only in connection with a white-and-green, or white-and-yellow beacon display, respectively.

6. Describe several types of aviation obstruction lighting. (AIM 2-2-3)

a. *Aviation red obstruction lights*—Flashing aviation red beacons and steady burning aviation red lights.

b. *High intensity white obstruction lights*—Flashing high intensity white lights during daytime with reduced intensity for twilight and nighttime operation.

c. *Dual lighting*—A combination of flashing aviation red beacons and steady burning aviation red lights for nighttime operation and flashing high intensity white lights for daytime operation.

7. What color are runway edge lights? (AIM 2-1-4)

Runway edge lights are white. On instrument runways, however, yellow replaces white on the last 2,000 feet or half the runway length, whichever is less, to form a caution zone for landings.

8. What color are the lights marking the ends of the runway? (AIM 2-1-4)

The lights marking the ends of the runway emit red light toward the runway to indicate the end of the runway to a departing aircraft, and green light outward from the runway end to indicate the threshold to landing aircraft.

9. Describe runway end identifier lights (REIL). (AIM 2-1-3)

REILs are installed at many airfields to provide rapid and positive identification of the approach end of a particular runway. The system consists of a pair of synchronized flashing lights located laterally on each side of the runway threshold. REIL may be either omnidirectional or unidirectional facing the approach area.

10. What color are taxiway edge lights? (AIM 2-1-10)

Taxiway edge lights emit blue light and are used to outline the edges of taxiways during periods of darkness or restricted visibility conditions.

11. What color are taxiway centerline lights? (AIM 2-1-10)

Taxiway centerline lights are steady-burning, green light.

12. How does a pilot determine the status of a light system at a particular airport? (FAA-H-8083-3)

The pilot needs to check the A/FD and any NOTAMs to find out about available lighting systems, light intensities and radio-controlled light system frequencies.

13. How does a pilot activate a radio-controlled runway light system while airborne? (AIM 2-1-8)

The pilot activates radio-controlled lights by keying the microphone on a specified frequency. The following sequence can be used for typical radio-controlled lighting systems:

a. On initial arrival, key the microphone seven times to turn the lights on and achieve maximum brightness;

b. If the runway lights are already on upon arrival, repeat the above sequence to ensure a full 15 minutes of lighting; then

c. The intensity of the lights can be adjusted by keying the microphone 7, 5, or 3 times within 5 seconds.

G. High-Altitude Operations

1. What are some basic operational advantages when conducting high-altitude operations?

a. True airspeeds increase with altitude

b. Winds aloft are stronger providing tailwind opportunities

c. Capability to see and avoid thunderstorms

d. Better visibility

e. Less turbulence

f. Above the weather instead of in it

g. Reduced chance for icing

h. Conflicts with other air traffic reduced

2. What are the regulations concerning use of supplemental oxygen on board an aircraft? (14 CFR 91.211)

No person may operate a civil aircraft of U.S. registry:

a. At cabin pressure altitudes above 12,500 feet MSL up to and including 14,000 feet MSL, unless, for that part of the flight at those altitudes that is more than 30 minutes, the required minimum flight crew is provided with and uses supplemental oxygen.

b. At cabin pressure altitudes above 14,000 feet MSL, unless the required flight crew is provided with and uses supplemental oxygen for the entire flight time at those altitudes.

c. At cabin pressure altitudes above 15,000 feet MSL, unless each occupant is provided with supplemental oxygen.

3. **What are the regulations pertaining to the use of supplemental oxygen on board a "pressurized" aircraft?** (14 CFR 91.211)

    Above Flight Level 250:

    At least a ten-minute supply of supplemental oxygen, in addition to any oxygen required to satisfy 14 CFR §91.211, is available for each occupant of the aircraft for use in the event that a descent is necessitated by loss of cabin pressurization.

    Above Flight Level 350:

    At least one pilot at the controls of the airplane is wearing and using an oxygen mask that is secured and sealed that either supplies oxygen at all times or automatically supplies oxygen whenever the cabin pressure altitude of the airplane exceeds 14,000 feet (MSL).

    Note: One pilot need not wear and use an oxygen mask while at or below Flight Level 410 if two pilots are at the controls and each pilot has a quick donning type of oxygen mask that can be placed on the face within 5 seconds. Also, if for any reason at any time it is necessary for one pilot to leave the controls of the aircraft when operating at altitudes above Flight Level 350, the remaining pilot at the controls shall put on and use an oxygen mask until the other pilot has returned to that crewmember's station.

4. **What are the requirements to operate within Class A airspace?** (14 CFR 91.135)

    a. Operated under IFR at a specific flight level assigned by ATC;

    b. Equipped with instruments and equipment required for IFR operations;

    c. Flown by a pilot rated for instrument flight; and

    d. Equipped, when in Class A airspace, with:
       - A radio providing direct pilot/controller communication on the frequency specified by ATC in the area concerned; and
       - The applicable equipment specified in 14 CFR §91.215 (transponder regulations).

5. **What additional equipment is required when operating above Flight Level 240?** (14 CFR 91.205)

   For flight at and above 24,000 feet MSL: if VOR navigational equipment is required (appropriate to the ground facilities to be used) no person may operate a U.S.-registered civil aircraft within the 50 states and the District of Columbia at or above FL240 unless that aircraft is equipped with approved distance measuring equipment (DME) or a suitable RNAV system.

6. **What type of navigational charts are used when operating at altitudes above 18,000 feet?** (AIM 9-1-4)

   Enroute high altitude charts are designed for navigation at or above 18,000 feet MSL. This four-color chart series includes the jet-route structure; VHF NAVAIDs with frequency identification, channel, geographic coordinates; selected airports, reporting points. These charts are revised every 56 days.

H. National Transportation Safety Board

1. **When is immediate notification to the NTSB required?** (NTSB Part 830)

   The operator of an aircraft shall immediately, and by the most expeditious means available, notify the nearest NTSB field office when an aircraft accident or any of the following listed incidents occur:

   a. Flight control system malfunction

   b. Crewmember unable to perform normal duties

   c. Turbine engine failure of structural components

   d. In-flight fire

   e. Aircraft collision in-flight

   f. Property damage, other than aircraft, estimated to exceed $25,000

   g. Overdue aircraft (believed to be in an accident)

2. After an accident or incident has occurred, how soon must a report be filed with the NTSB? (NTSB Part 830)

The operator shall file a report on NTSB Form 6120.1 or 6120.2, available from NTSB field offices or from the NTSB, Washington D.C., 20594:

a. Within 10 days after an accident;

b. When, after 7 days, an overdue aircraft is still missing.

A report on an "Incident" for which notification is required as described shall be filed only as requested by an authorized representative of the NTSB.

3. Define aircraft accident. (NTSB Part 830.2)

An aircraft accident means an occurrence associated with the operation of an aircraft which takes place between the time any person boards the aircraft with the intention of flight and all such persons have disembarked, and in which any person suffers death or serious injury, or in which the aircraft receives substantial damage.

4. Define aircraft incident. (NTSB Part 830.2)

An aircraft incident means an occurrence other than an accident associated with the operation of an aircraft, which affects or could affect the safety of operations.

5. Define the term serious injury. (NTSB Part 830.2)

Serious injury means any injury which:

a. Requires hospitalization for more than 48 hours, commencing within 7 days from the date the injury was received;

b. Results in a fracture of any bone (except simple fractures of fingers, toes or nose);

c. Causes severe hemorrhages, nerve, muscle or tendon damage;

d. Involves any internal organ; or

e. Involves second- or third-degree burns affecting more than 5% of the body surface.

6. Define the term substantial damage. (NTSB Part 830.2)

Substantial damage means damage or failure which adversely affects structural strength, performance or flight characteristics of the aircraft and which normally requires major repair or replacement of the affected component.

7. Will notification to the NTSB always be necessary in any aircraft "accident" even if there were no injuries? (NTSB Part 830)

Refer to the definition of "accident." An aircraft accident can be substantial damage and/or injuries, and the NTSB always requires a report if this is the case.

8. Where are accident or incident reports filed? (NTSB Part 830)

The operator of an aircraft shall file any report with the field office of the Board nearest the accident or incident. The National Transportation Safety Board field offices are listed in the U.S. government pages of telephone directories in major cities.

Continued...

Additional Study Questions

1. **What types of airspace is categorized as "Other" airspace?** (AIM 3-5-1 through 3-5-7)

2. **What wind condition prolongs the hazards of wake turbulence on a landing runway for the longest period of time?** (AIM 7-3-4)

3. **What situation would result in "reverse sensing" of a VOR receiver?** (FAA-H-8083-25)

4. **What is the main difference between controlled airspace and uncontrolled airspace?** (AIM 3-2-1 and 3-3-1)

5. **Do regulations permit a pilot to drop objects from an aircraft in flight?** (14 CFR 91.15)

6. **When a control tower closes, the airspace within the airport surface area reverts from Class D airspace to Class E airspace. How will this affect the VFR weather minimums?** (AIM 3-2-5)

7. **When transitioning busy terminal airspace, where can information be found concerning VFR flyways, corridors and transition routes?** (AIM 3-5-5)

8. **What is the width of a federal airway?** (FAA-H-8083-15)

9. **What significance does an underlined VOR station frequency have on a VFR sectional chart?** (FAA-H-8083-25)

10. **When would a pilot use the following charts: WAC charts; TAC charts; Sectional charts?** (AIM 9-1-4)

ADM and CRM   **7**

A. Aeronautical Decision Making

1. Define aeronautical decision making (ADM). (FAA-H-8083-9)

ADM is the systematic approach to the mental process used by aircraft pilots to consistently determine the best course of action in response to a given set of circumstances.

2. During flight, decisions must be made regarding events that involve interactions between the four risk elements. What are they? (FAA-H-8083-9)

Pilot in command – the aircraft – the environment – the operation

3. The DECIDE model for decision making involves which elements? (FAA-H-8083-25)

D etect a change needing attention.
E stimate the need to counter or react to change.
C hoose the most desirable outcome for the flight.
I dentify actions to successfully control the change.
D o something to adapt to the change.
E valuate the effect of the action countering the change.

4. What are the major factors affecting judgment and decision making? (FAA-H-8083-9)

Stress – health – attitude – experience

5. Name the five hazardous attitudes that negatively impact a pilot's judgment and ability to make competent decisions and their antidotes. (FAA-H-8083-9)

Attitudes	Antidotes
Anti-authority	Follow the rules, they are usually right.
Impulsivity	Think first — not so fast.
Invulnerability	It could happen to me.
Macho	Taking chances is foolish.
Resignation	I can make a difference, I am not helpless.

B. Crew Resource Management

1. What does crew resource management (CRM) refer to? (FAA-H-8083-9)

CRM is the application of team management concepts in the flight deck environment. It was initially known as "cockpit resource management," but as CRM programs evolved to include cabin crews, maintenance personnel, and others, it became "crew resource management." This includes single pilots, as in most general aviation aircraft. Pilots of small aircraft, as well as crews of larger aircraft, must make effective use of all available resources; human resources, hardware, and information.

2. Which groups routinely working with the cockpit crew may also be viewed as effective components of CRM and the decision making process in the cockpit? (FAA-H-8083-9)

All groups routinely working with the cockpit crew who are involved in decisions required to operate a flight safely. These groups include, but are not limited to pilots, dispatchers, cabin crewmembers, maintenance personnel, and air traffic controllers. CRM is one way of addressing the challenge of optimizing the human/machine interface and accompanying interpersonal activities.

3. Discuss the importance of understanding the concept of positive exchange of flight controls, as it relates to flight training. (FAA-H-8083-9)

During flight training, there must always be a clear understanding between students and flight instructors of who has control of the aircraft. Prior to flight, a briefing should be conducted that includes the procedure for the exchange of flight controls. A positive three-step process in the exchange of flight controls between pilots is a proven procedure and one that is strongly recommended.

4. **Describe the three-step process used for the positive exchange of flight controls.** (FAA-H-8083-9)

During this procedure, a visual check is recommended to see that the other person actually has the flight controls. When returning the controls to the instructor, the student should follow the same procedure the instructor used when giving control to the student. The student should stay on the controls and keep flying the aircraft until the instructor says, "I have the flight controls." There should never be any doubt as to who is flying the aircraft:

- When the flight instructor wishes the student to take control of the aircraft, the instructor says to the student: "You have the flight controls."
- The student acknowledges immediately by saying: "I have the flight controls."
- The flight instructor again says: "You have the flight controls."

C. Situational Awareness

1. **What is situational awareness?** (FAA-H-8083-9)

It is the accurate perception and understanding of all the factors and conditions within the four fundamental risk elements affecting safety before, during, and after the flight.

2. **Situational awareness takes into consideration which four elements?** (FAA-H-8083-9)

The four elements to be taken into consideration with situational awareness are:

Pilot—Aircraft—Environment—Type of Operation—
and their interaction with each other.

3. **What are some of the elements, both inside and outside the aircraft, that a pilot must consider in order to maintain situational awareness?** (FAA-H-8083-9)

Inside aircraft—status of aircraft systems, pilots, and passengers.

Outside aircraft—environmental conditions of the flight, spatial orientation of the aircraft, relationship to surrounding terrain, traffic, weather and airspace.

4. **What are some of the obstacles to maintaining situational awareness?** (FAA-H-8083-9)

Fatigue, stress, and work overload can cause the pilot to fixate on a single perceived important item rather than maintaining an overall awareness of the flight situation. A contributing factor in many accidents is a distraction, which diverts the pilot's attention from monitoring the instruments or scanning outside the aircraft. Many cockpit distractions begin as a minor problem, such as a gauge that is not reading correctly, but result in accidents as the pilot diverts attention to the perceived problem and neglects to properly control the aircraft.

5. **What are "operational pitfalls"?** (FAA-H-8083-9)

There are a number of classic behavioral traps into which pilots have been known to fall. Pilots, particularly those with considerable experience, as a rule always try to complete a flight as planned, please passengers, meet schedules, and generally demonstrate that they have the "right stuff." The basic drive to demonstrate the right stuff can have an adverse effect on safety, and can impose an unrealistic assessment of piloting skills under stressful conditions. These tendencies ultimately may bring about practices that are dangerous and often illegal, and may lead to a mishap.

6. What are some examples of operational pitfalls that pilots have been known to experience? (FAA-H-8083-9)

a. Peer pressure

b. Mindset

c. Get-There-Itis

d. Duck-under syndrome/Descent below minimums

e. Scud running

f. Continuing visual flight rules (VFR) into instrument conditions

g. Getting behind the aircraft

h. Loss of positional or situational awareness

i. Operating without adequate fuel reserves

j. Descent below the minimum enroute altitude

k. Flying outside the envelope

l. Neglect of flight planning, preflight inspections, and checklists

D. Use of Checklists

1. Why are pilots encouraged to use checklists?
(FAA-H-8083-3)

Checklists provide a logical and standardized method to operate a particular make and model airplane. Following a checklist reinforces the use of proper procedures throughout all major phases of flight operations.

2. What are the two primary methods for using checklists?

a. Read and Do: This is when the pilot picks up a checklist, refers to an item, and sets the condition. The items for any particular phase of flight would all be accomplished before the checklist is set aside.

b. Do and Verify: Set the condition of the items for a particular phase of operation from memory or flow pattern, then use the checklist and read to verify that the appropriate condition for each item in that phase has been set. It is not wise for a pilot to become so reliant upon a flow pattern that he or she fails to verify with a checklist. Checking important items solely from memory is not an acceptable substitute for checklists.

3. What are some examples of checklists a pilot will use in the course of a flight? (FAA-H-8083-3)

a. Preflight Inspection

b. Before Engine Starting

c. Use of External Power

d. Engine Starting

e. Before Taxiing

f. Before Takeoff

g. Climb

h. Cruise

i. Descent

j. Before Landing

k. Balked Landing

l. After Landing

m. Shutdown

n. Postflight/ELT Check

Additional Study Questions

1. What represents the first basic element in good decision making? (FAA-H-8083-9)

2. What criteria may a pilot use when evaluating flying risks? (FAA-H-8083-9)

3. Describe the three stressors representing a barrier to effective decision making. (FAA-H-8083-9)

4. Most of the hazards in flying can be minimized by adopting what general philosophy? (FAA-H-8083-9)

5. What role does complacency have in reducing a pilot's situational awareness? (FAA-H-8083-9)

6. Good CRM involves leadership. What are some of the qualities a pilot should possess to be an effective leader? (FAA-H-8083-9)

7. What is the significance of "immediate action items" found on some checklists? (Order 8900.1)

8. Why should pilots reference the actual emergency checklist after completion of the immediate action items? (Order 8900.1)

Aeromedical Factors

8

A. Fitness for Flight

1. What regulations apply to medical certification?

Part 67 — Medical Standards and Certification.

2. As a flight crewmember, you discover you have high blood pressure. You are in possession of a current medical certificate. Can you continue to exercise the privileges of your certificate? (AIM 8-1-1)

No, the regulations prohibit a pilot who possesses a current medical certificate from performing crewmember duties while the pilot has a known medical condition or an increase of a known medical condition that would make the pilot unable to meet the standards for the medical certificate.

3. Are flight crewmembers allowed the use of any medications while performing required duties? (AIM 8-1-1)

The regulations prohibit pilots from performing crewmember duties while using any medication that affects the faculties in any way contrary to safety. The safest rule is not to fly as a crewmember while taking any medication, unless approved to do so by the FAA.

4. Are there any over-the-counter medications that could be considered safe to use while flying? (AIM 8-1-1)

No; pilot performance can be seriously degraded by both prescribed and over-the-counter medications, as well as by the medical conditions for which they are taken. Many medications have primary effects that may impair judgment, memory, alertness, coordination, vision, and the ability to make calculations. Also, any medication that depresses the central nervous system can make a pilot more susceptible to hypoxia.

5. What are several factors which may contribute to impairment of a pilot's performance? (AIM 8-1-1)

I llness
M edication
S tress
A lcohol
F atigue
E motion

B. Flight Physiology

1. What is hypoxia? (AIM 8-1-2)

Hypoxia is a state of oxygen deficiency in the body sufficient to impair functions of the brain and other organs.

2. Where does hypoxia usually occur, and what symptoms should one expect? (AIM 8-1-2)

Although a deterioration in night vision occurs at a cabin pressure altitude as low as 5,000 feet, other significant effects of altitude hypoxia usually do not occur in the normal healthy pilot below 12,000 feet. From 12,000 feet to 15,000 feet of altitude, judgment, memory, alertness, coordination, and ability to make calculations are impaired, and headache, drowsiness, dizziness and either a sense of well-being or belligerence occur.

3. What factors can make a pilot more susceptible to hypoxia? (AIM 8-1-2)

a. Carbon monoxide inhaled in smoking or from exhaust fumes.

b. Anemia (lowered hemoglobin)

c. Certain medications

d. Small amounts of alcohol

e. Low doses of certain drugs (antihistamines, tranquilizers, sedatives, analgesics, etc.)

Also, extreme heat or cold, fever, and anxiety increase the body's demand for oxygen, and hence its susceptibility to hypoxia.

4. How can hypoxia be avoided? (AIM 8-1-2)

Hypoxia is prevented by heeding factors that reduce tolerance to altitude; by enriching the inspired air with oxygen from an appropriate oxygen system; and by maintaining a comfortable, safe cabin pressure altitude. For optimum protection, pilots are encouraged to use supplemental oxygen above 10,000 feet during the day and above 5,000 feet at night.

5. What is hyperventilation? (AIM 8-1-3)

Hyperventilation, or an abnormal increase in the volume of air breathed in and out of the lungs, can occur subconsciously when a stressful situation is encountered in flight. This results in a significant decrease in the carbon dioxide content of the blood. Carbon dioxide is needed to automatically regulate the breathing process.

6. What symptoms can a pilot expect from hyperventilation? (AIM 8-1-3)

As hyperventilation "blows off" excessive carbon dioxide from the body, a pilot can experience symptoms of lightheadedness, suffocation, drowsiness, tingling in the extremities, and coolness, and react to them with even greater hyperventilation. Incapacitation can eventually result from uncoordination, disorientation, and painful muscle spasms. Finally, unconsciousness can occur.

7. How can a hyperventilating condition be reversed? (AIM 8-1-3)

The symptoms of hyperventilation subside within a few minutes after the rate and depth of breathing are consciously brought back under control. The buildup of carbon dioxide in the body can be hastened by controlled breathing in and out of a paper bag held over the nose and mouth.

8. What is ear block? (AIM 8-1-2)

As the aircraft cabin pressure decreases during ascent, the expanding air in the middle ear pushes open the Eustachian tube and escapes down to the nasal passages, thereby equalizing in pressure with the cabin pressure. But this isn't automatic during descent, and the pilot must periodically open the Eustachian tube to equalize pressure. An upper respiratory infection or a nasal allergic condition can produce enough congestion around the Eustachian tube to make equalization difficult. Consequently, the difference in pressure between the middle ear and aircraft cabin can build to a level that holds the Eustachian tube closed, making equalization difficult if not impossible. An ear block produces severe pain and loss of hearing that can last from several hours to several days.

9. How is ear block normally prevented from occurring? (AIM 8-1-2)

Normally this can be accomplished by swallowing, yawning, tensing muscles in the throat or, if these do not work, by the combination of closing the mouth, pinching the nose closed and attempting to blow through the nostrils (Valsalva maneuver). It is also prevented by not flying with an upper respiratory infection or nasal allergic condition.

10. What is spatial disorientation? (FAA-H-8083-15)

Orientation is the awareness of the position of the aircraft and of oneself in relation to a specific reference point. Spatial disorientation specifically refers to the lack of orientation with regard to position in space and to other objects.

11. What causes spatial disorientation? (FAA-H-8083-15)

Orientation is maintained through the body's sensory organs in three areas:

a. Visual: the eyes maintain visual orientation;

b. Vestibular: the motion sensing system in the inner ear maintains vestibular orientation;

c. Postural: the nerves in the skin, joints, and muscles of the body maintain postural orientation.

When human beings are in their natural environment, these three systems work well. However, when the human body is subjected to the forces of flight, these senses can provide misleading information resulting in disorientation.

12. What is the cause of motion sickness, and what are its symptoms? (FAA-P-8740-41)

Motion sickness is caused by continued stimulation of the tiny portion of the inner ear which controls the pilot's sense of balance. The symptoms are progressive. First, the desire for food is lost. Then saliva collects in the mouth and the person begins to perspire freely. Eventually, he or she becomes nauseated and disoriented. The head aches and there may be a tendency to vomit. If the air sickness becomes severe enough, the pilot may become completely incapacitated.

13. What action should be taken if a pilot or passenger suffers from motion sickness? (FAA-P-8740-41)

If suffering from airsickness while piloting an aircraft, open up the air vents, loosen the clothing, use supplemental oxygen, and keep the eyes on a point outside the airplane. Avoid unnecessary head movements. Then cancel the flight and land as soon as possible.

14. What regulations apply, and what common sense should prevail concerning the use of alcohol? (AIM 8-1-1)

The regulations prohibit pilots from performing crewmember duties within 8 hours after drinking any alcoholic beverage or while under the influence of alcohol. However, due to the slow destruction of alcohol, a pilot may still be under influence 8 hours after drinking a moderate amount of alcohol. Therefore, an excellent rule is to allow at least 12 to 24 hours from "bottle to throttle," depending on the amount of alcoholic beverage consumed.

15. What is carbon monoxide poisoning? (AIM 8-1-4)

Carbon monoxide is a colorless, odorless and tasteless gas contained in exhaust fumes. When breathed, even in minute quantities over a period of time, it can significantly reduce the ability of the blood to carry oxygen. Consequently, effects of hypoxia occur.

16. How does carbon monoxide poisoning occur, and what symptoms should a pilot be alert for? (AIM 8-1-4)

Most heaters in light aircraft work by air flowing over the manifold. Use of these heaters while exhaust fumes are escaping through manifold cracks and seals is responsible for several nonfatal and fatal aircraft accidents from carbon monoxide poisoning each year. A pilot who detects the odor of exhaust or experiences symptoms of headache, drowsiness, or dizziness while using the heater should suspect carbon monoxide poisoning.

17. What action should be taken if a pilot suspects carbon monoxide poisoning? (AIM 8-1-4)

A pilot who suspects this condition to exist should immediately shut off the heater and open all air vents. If symptoms are severe, or continue after landing, medical treatment should be sought.

18. What precautions should be taken before flight if you or your passengers have been involved in recent scuba diving activity? (AIM 8-1-2)

A pilot or passenger who intends to fly after scuba diving should allow the body sufficient time to rid itself of excess nitrogen absorbed during diving. If not, decompression sickness due to evolved gas can occur during exposure to higher altitudes and create a serious inflight emergency.

The recommended waiting time before flight to cabin pressure altitudes of 8,000 feet or less is at least 12 hours after diving which has not required controlled ascent (non-decompression diving) and at least 24 hours after diving which has required controlled ascent (decompression diving). The waiting time before flight to cabin pressure altitudes above 8,000 feet should be at least 24 hours after any scuba diving.

Additional Study Questions

1. What is acute fatigue? Chronic fatigue? (AIM 8-1-1)

2. What is stress? (AIM 8-1-1)

3. What are some examples of the different types of spatial disorientation? (AIM 8-1-5)

4. How can spatial disorientation be prevented? (AIM 8-1-5)

5. What is the difference between anemic hypoxia and hypoxic hypoxia? (AIM 8-1-2)

6. What are examples of specific drugs that have been associated with aircraft accidents in the past? (FAA-P-8740-41)

7. How can a pilot detect the presence of carbon monoxide in the cockpit? (FAA-P-8740-41)

8. What is sinus block? (AIM 8-1-2)

9. Rain on the windshield of an aircraft on approach to landing will produce what type of illusion? (AIM 8-1-5)

10. What actions can you take to reduce the chances that a passenger will suffer from motion sickness? (FAA-H-8083-25)

Commercial
Flight
Maneuvers   **9**

A. Steep Turns

1. What is a steep turn? (FAA-H-8083-3)

Steep turns are those resulting from a degree of bank (more than approximately 45 degrees) at which the overbanking tendency of an airplane overcomes stability, and the bank tends to increase unless pressure is applied to the aileron controls to prevent it. Maximum turning performance is attained and relatively high load factors are imposed.

2. What is the desired bank angle in a steep turn? (FAA-S-8081-12)

A bank angle of at least 50° (±5°) is desired.

3. What is the recommended entry speed for a steep turn? (FAA-S-8081-12)

Establish the manufacturer's recommended airspeed or if one is not stated, a safe airspeed not to exceed V_A.

4. How do you maintain altitude in a steep turn? (FAA-H-8083-3)

To maintain altitude, as well as orientation, requires an awareness of the relative position of the nose, the horizon, the wings, and the amount of bank. If the altitude begins to increase, or decrease, relaxing or increasing the back-elevator pressure will be required as appropriate. This may also require a power adjustment to maintain the selected airspeed. A small increase or decrease of 1° to 3° of bank angle may be used to control small altitude deviations.

5. What are the altitude, airspeed, bank, and heading tolerances for a steep turn? (FAA-S-8081-12)

Maintain the entry altitude, ±100 feet (30 meters), airspeed, ±10 knots, bank, ±5°; and roll out on the entry heading, ±10°.

B. Chandelles

1. What is a chandelle? (FAA-H-8083-3)

A "chandelle" is a maximum performance climbing turn beginning from approximately straight and level flight, and ending at the completion of 180° of turn in a wings-level, nose-high attitude at the minimum controllable airspeed.

2. In a chandelle, constant bank and changing pitch occur in what part of the maneuver? (FAA-H-8083-3)

The first 90° of turn require a constant 30° of bank and a gradual and constant change in pitch attitude.

3. In a chandelle, constant pitch and changing bank occur in what part of the maneuver? (FAA-H-8083-3)

The last 90° of turn requires a very gradual change in bank from 30° to 0° and a constant pitch attitude so as to arrive at minimum airspeed as the airplane is rolled out to a wings-level attitude.

4. What is the maximum amount of bank in the chandelle? (FAA-S-8081-12)

30° of bank.

5. What should your speed be upon completion of the chandelle? (FAA-S-8081-12)

You should begin a coordinated constant-rate rollout from the 90° point to the 180° point, ±10° just above a stall airspeed, and maintaining that airspeed momentarily avoiding a stall.

6. At what two points will your wings be level in a chandelle? (FAA-S-8081-12)

Immediately before entering the chandelle and upon rollout at the 180° point.

C. Lazy Eights

1. What is a lazy eight? (FAA-H-8083-3)

A lazy eight consists of two 180° turns, in opposite directions, while making a climb and a descent in a symmetrical pattern during each of the turns.

2. What procedures are recommended prior to beginning a lazy-eight maneuver? (FAA-H-8083-3)

Prior to performing a lazy eight, the airspace behind and above should be clear of other air traffic. The maneuver should be entered from straight-and-level flight at normal cruise power and at the airspeed recommended by the manufacturer or at the airplane's design maneuvering speed.

3. Where should the highest pitch attitude occur in a lazy eight? (FAA-H-8083-3)

At the 45° point the pitch attitude should be at a maximum and the angle of bank continuing to increase. Also, at the 45° point, the pitch attitude should start to decrease slowly toward the horizon at the 90° reference point.

4. Where should the lowest nose-down attitude occur in a lazy eight? (FAA-H-8083-3)

When the airplane has turned 135°, the nose should be at its lowest pitch attitude.

5. What are the altitude, airspeed and heading tolerances allowed when performing a lazy eight? (FAA-S-8081-12)

You should achieve the following throughout the maneuver:

a. Approximately 30° bank at the steepest point.

b. Constant change of pitch and roll rate.

c. Altitude tolerance at 180° points, ±100 feet (30 meters) from entry altitude.

d. Airspeed tolerance at the 180° point, ±10° knots from entry airspeed.

e. Heading tolerance at the 180° point, ±10°.

6. To summarize, describe the appropriate values to be obtained in a lazy eight at the entry, 45-, 90-, 135- and 180-degree points. (FAA-H-8083-3)

Entry
— Level flight
— Maneuvering or cruise speed (whichever is less) or manufacturer's recommended speed

45° point
— Maximum pitch-up attitude
— Bank angle at 15°

90° point
— Bank angle approximately 30°
— Minimum airspeed
— Maximum altitude
— Level pitch attitude

135° point
— Maximum pitch-down attitude
— Bank approximately 15°

180° point
— Level flight
— Original heading (±10°)
— Entry airspeed (±10 knots)
— Entry altitude (±100 feet)

D. Eights-On-Pylons

1. What are eights-on-pylons? (FAA-H-8083-3)

Eights-on-pylons is a training maneuver that involves flying the airplane in circular paths, alternately left and right, in the form of a figure-8 around two selected points or pylons on the ground. No attempt is made to maintain a uniform distance from the pylon. Instead, the airplane is flown at such an altitude and airspeed that a line parallel to the airplane's lateral axis, and extending from the pilot's eye appears to pivot on each of the pylons.

2. How do you determine pivotal altitude for eights-on-pylons? (FAA-H-8083-3)

An entry pivotal altitude value is initially calculated by using the ground speed entering the maneuver. Since the first turn is made into the wind, this will be the slowest ground speed. Use the formula:

If airspeed indicator is in MPH:

$$GS^2 \div 15 = PA$$

If airspeed indicator is in KNOTS:

$$GS^2 \div 11.3 = PA$$

3. Does the pivotal altitude change in eights-on-pylons? (FAA-H-8083-3)

Yes, the pivotal altitude is critical and will change with variations in ground speed. Since the headings throughout the turns continually vary from directly downwind to directly upwind, the ground speed will constantly change. This will result in the proper pivotal altitude varying slightly throughout the eight. Therefore, adjustment must be made for this by climbing and descending as necessary to hold the reference line or point on the pylons. This change in altitude will be dependent on how much the wind affects the ground speed.

Remember...

Ground speed goes UP, Pivotal Altitude goes UP.

Ground speed goes DOWN, Pivotal Altitude goes DOWN.

4. How far should one pylon be from the other pylon in eights-on-pylons? (FAA-S-8081-12)

They should be of sufficient distance apart to permit straight and level flight between pylons.

5. Where is the highest pivotal altitude likely to occur in eights-on-pylons? (FAA-H-8083-3)

As the airplane turns downwind the ground speed increases; consequently the pivotal altitude is higher and the airplane must climb to hold the reference line on the pylon.

6. Where is the lowest pivotal altitude likely to occur in eights-on-pylons? (FAA-H-8083-3)

As the airplane heads into the wind, the ground speed decreases; consequently the pivotal altitude is lower and the airplane must descend to hold the reference line on the pylon.

7. What action should you take if your wing reference point appears to move ahead of the pylon? Move behind the pylon? (FAA-H-8083-3)

If the reference line appears to move ahead of the pylon, the pilot should increase altitude. If the reference line appears to move behind the pylon, the pilot should decrease altitude. Varying rudder pressure to yaw the airplane and force the wing and reference line forward or backward to the pylon is a dangerous technique and must not be attempted.

E. Power-Off 180° Accuracy Approach and Landing

1. What is a power-off 180° accuracy approach and landing? (FAA-H-8083-3)

Power-off accuracy approaches and landings are made by gliding, with the engine idling, from a specific point on downwind to touchdown, in a normal landing attitude at or within 200 feet beyond the specified touchdown point.

2. State the objective of learning a power-off 180° accuracy approach and landing. (FAA-H-8083-3)

Its objective is to further develop judgment in estimating distances and glide ratios, in that the airplane is flown without power from a higher altitude and through a 90° turn to reach the base-leg position at a proper altitude for executing the 90° approach.

3. What are the standards expected of a student when executing this type of approach and landing? (FAA-S-8081-12)

The student must:

a. Exhibit knowledge of the elements related to a power-off 180° accuracy approach and landing.

b. Consider the wind conditions, landing surface, obstructions, and selects an appropriate touchdown point.

c. Position airplane on downwind leg, parallel to landing runway, and not more than 1,000 feet AGL.

d. Abeam the specified touchdown point, close throttle and establish appropriate glide speed.

e. Complete final airplane configuration.

f. Touch down in a normal landing attitude, at or within 200 feet (60 meters) beyond the specified touchdown point.

g. Complete the appropriate checklist.

F. Steep Spirals

1. What is a steep spiral? (FAA-H-8083-3)

A steep spiral is nothing more than a constant gliding turn, during which a constant radius around a point on the ground is maintained similar to the maneuver "turns around a point." The radius should be such that the steepest bank will not exceed 60°.

2. What is the objective of a steep spiral? (FAA-H-8083-3)

The objective of this maneuver is to improve pilot techniques for airspeed control, wind drift control, planning, orientation, and division of attention. The steep spiral is not only a valuable flight training maneuver, but has practical application by providing a procedure for dissipating altitude while remaining over a selected spot in preparation for landing, especially for emergency forced landings.

3. What standards must you maintain when executing a steep spiral? (FAA-S-8081-12)

Start at an altitude that will allow a series of three 360°-turns. Maintain the specified airspeed ±10 knots, roll out toward object or specified heading ±10°, and do not exceed 60° of bank while applying wind drift correction to track a constant radius circle around a defined reference point.

Additional Study Questions

1. Why does the airplane have a tendency to overbank in a steep turn? (FAA-H-8083-3)

2. What effect will a steep turn have on an airplane's stall speed and load factor? Why? (FAA-H-8083-3)

3. Discuss the potential outcome of the chandelle maneuver if you use too much pitch initially; not enough pitch initially. (FAA-H-8083-3)

4. What altitude and airspeed will you use when entering a chandelle? (FAA-H-8083-3)

5. When entering a lazy eight, will you establish the bank first, pitch first, or both at the same time? (FAA-H-8083-3)

6. Discuss reference point selection for the lazy eight maneuver. (FAA-H-8083-3)

7. When performing a lazy eight, why is more right rudder required in the right turn than in the left turn? (FAA-H-8083-3)

8. When performing an eights-on-pylon maneuver, where will the steepest angle of bank occur? (FAA-H-8083-3)

9. Will the pivotal altitude change when changing the angle-of-bank in an eights-on-pylon maneuver? (FAA-H-8083-3)

10. What initial altitude and airspeed will you use when entering an eights-on-pylon maneuver? (FAA-H-8083-3)

Applicant's Practical Test Checklist

Appendix

Applicant's Practical Test Checklist

Appointment with Examiner

Examiner's Name _____

Location _____

Date and Time _____

Acceptable Aircraft

Aircraft Documents

___ Airworthiness Certificate

___ Registration Certificate

___ Operating Limitations

Aircraft Maintenance Records

___ Logbook record of airworthiness inspections and AD compliance

___ Pilot's Operating Handbook, FAA-approved Airplane Flight Manual

___ Current weight and balance data

Personal Equipment

___ View-limiting device

___ Current aeronautical charts

___ Computer and plotter

___ Flight plan form

___ Flight logs

___ Current AIM, Airport/Facility Directory, and appropriate publications

Personal Records

___ Identification—Photo/Signature ID

___ Pilot certificate

___ Current and appropriate medical certificate

___ Completed FAA Form 8710-1, airman certificate and/or rating application with instructor's signature (if applicable)

___ Computer test report

___ Pilot logbook with appropriate instructor endorsements

___ FAA Form 8060-5, Notice of Disapproval (if applicable)

___ Approved school graduation certificate (if applicable)

___ Examiner's fee (if applicable)

Notes

Notes

Notes

Notes